MW01113377

Writing the Revolution

WRITING THE REVOLUTION

A French Woman's History in Letters

LINDSAY A. H. PARKER

OXFORD
UNIVERSITY PRESS

OXFORD
UNIVERSITY PRESS

Oxford University Press is a department of the University of Oxford.
It furthers the University's objective of excellence in research, scholarship,
and education by publishing worldwide.

Oxford   New York
Auckland   Cape Town   Dar es Salaam   Hong Kong   Karachi
Kuala Lumpur   Madrid   Melbourne   Mexico City   Nairobi
New Delhi   Shanghai   Taipei   Toronto

With offices in
Argentina   Austria   Brazil   Chile   Czech Republic   France   Greece
Guatemala   Hungary   Italy   Japan   Poland   Portugal   Singapore
South Korea   Switzerland   Thailand   Turkey   Ukraine   Vietnam

Oxford is a registered trademark of Oxford University Press
in the UK and certain other countries.

© Oxford University Press 2013

Published in the United States of America by
Oxford University Press
198 Madison Avenue, New York, NY 10016

Library of Congress Cataloging-in-Publication Data
Parker, Lindsay A. H.
Writing the Revolution : a French woman's history in letters / Lindsay A.H. Parker
pages cm
Includes bibliographical references and index.
ISBN 978-0-19-993102-6 (hardback : acid-free paper)
1. Jullien, Rosalie—Correspondence.   2. Women—France—Correspondence.   3. Jullien,
Rosalie—Family.   4. France—History—Revolution, 1789–1799.   5. France—History—
1789–1815.   6. French letters—Women authors—History and criticism.   7. Letter writing,
French—History.   8. Women—France—History.   9. Paris (France)—History—
1789–1799.   10. Paris (France)—History—1799–1815.   I. Title.
DC146.J77P37 2013
944.04092—dc23
2012045394

For my parents,
Gary and Kathleen Holowach

I had thought that [the Revolution] would march under the banner of philosophy, without bloodshed, among a kind people who believed in universal fraternity. What a dream!

ROSALIE JULLIEN, April 29, 1793

Contents

Acknowledgments

THE GENEROUS SUPPORT of several academic institutions and societies assisted my research for this book. Travel grants from the Institute of European Studies at the University of California, Berkeley, and from the Humanities Research Center and the Center for Writing and Translation at the University of California, Irvine, sustained several trips to France. Similarly, an award from the Western Association of Women Historians helped me finish this project. Portions of this book have been published previously in the *Journal of Women's History*.

I extend thanks to all of the historians who shared their time with me in classes, conferences, and cafés. Deep gratitude goes to Timothy Tackett, an inspirational thesis director and an admirable scholar. I appreciated the opportunity to practice history with his guidance and thank him for putting me on Rosalie's path eight years ago. Thanks are due to Sarah Farmer, Robert Moeller, and Ulrike Strasser, who supported my efforts as a graduate student with thoughtful criticism and kind prompting. I am grateful for the friendship of Nina Gelbart, Margaret Darrow, and Helen Chenut.

I am indebted to genealogist Mary Kergall, the Bon family, and charming historians and hosts Jean Sauvageon and Claude Magnan. I hope that they feel this book warrants their great efforts. Working with Nancy Toff, Sonia Tycko, and the editors at Oxford University Press has been incredibly enjoyable, and I thank them for the energy they have put into this project.

My peers in graduate school contributed intellectual and personal camaraderie. They include Patricia Goldsworthy-Bishop, Angela Hawk, Christine Eubank, Nicole Labouf, Kurt MacMillan, and Kimberly

Weiss. I thank everyone who engaged with me in conversation, epistolary and otherwise, about my endeavor. Indeed, this work bears the impression of many kind and interesting people. While they are too numerous to list, I share my work's merit with them. Any errors, however, are my own.

I dedicate this book to my parents by way of thanking them for love and encouragement beyond the moon and the stars—indeed, beyond words. I wish also to remember my grandparents, whose stories inspired my imagination. The friendship of my dear sister Courtney Holowach brought cheer to many lonely corners of dim archives. Finally, to my husband, Andrew Parker, I owe my deepest thanks for being my constant companion from the beginning. I am so proud to be, above all, your loving wife.

Writing the Revolution

Introduction

IN THE PÈRE Lachaise cemetery in Paris, a few gravestones away from Frédéric Chopin's festooned resting place, a crumbling monument sits in shadow. The engraving on the chalky stone reads, "To Rosalie Ducrollay, widow Jullien. A mother's heart is the Creator's masterpiece." Rosalie died in 1824. For nearly two centuries, she has been an indistinguishable figure—the person behind an unknown name and one more grave in a field of people both famous and ordinary. Just as Rosalie often was, her gravestone is shaded and silent, concealing a noteworthy life. But in an obscure designation in the National Archives in Paris, the Archives privée, her life is revealed through a collection of nearly one thousand of her letters.

Rosalie Jullien's correspondence spans the period from 1775 through 1810. She wrote the majority of the letters during the French Revolution, which surrounded her as she lived in Paris. Although prolific, her writing was not usually meant for public consumption. She preferred to maintain privacy while still being patriotic. "There is a part of France that is stronger than those who decorate themselves with different names or parade with this or that faction. It is made of the imposing majority, those who have a just spirit and a right heart in the interior of their homes... [where] they judge men and kings," Rosalie wrote in a letter to her son on June 1, 1792.[1] According to her account, Rosalie was one of the majority in the French Revolution: a bourgeois wife and mother who celebrated the Revolution from within the home. If this group of patriots was substantial in number, it was also low in visibility. In fact, very little is known about the women who lived through the French Revolution of 1789. Her missives are among the scant traces of Rosalie, judge of kings.

Rosalie Ducrollay was born September 9, 1745, in Pontoise, not very far from Paris. Her father, Philippe, was a wholesale merchant and minor notable. He married her mother, Antoinette Jaquin, on February 12, 1743. Rosalie was the second of two children; her older sister, Charlotte, was born December 10, 1743. In 1775, Rosalie "married" Marc-Antoine Jullien—the complexities of this alliance will unfold shortly. Marc-Antoine was born April 18, 1744, to a surgeon in Romans, in Dauphiné. When he wed Rosalie, he was a recent widower and an aspiring man of letters. Rosalie and Marc-Antoine named their first child for his father, but they immediately called him Jules. For clarity, I do the same. When Auguste was born in September 1779, the family of four was complete.

While their children were young, Rosalie and Marc-Antoine lived in Romans. Throughout their decade in the country, Rosalie became adept at managing large amounts of farmland, raising silkworms, and especially cultivating a sentimental home with her husband and two children. The influences of Enlightenment literature are clear in their family interactions. Marc-Antoine was well-read in Jean-Jacques Rousseau's political commentaries as well as his romantic novels. Rousseau's ideas complemented those of Marc-Antoine's old friend the abbé Mably. While Rosalie was largely interested in literature that would help her raise virtuous children, Marc-Antoine hoped to become a successful man of letters and join the discourse on social issues. But neither Rosalie nor Marc-Antoine anticipated the Revolution.

The Jullien family moved to Paris in 1787. Once the Revolution began, they witnessed its major events, sometimes simply from the window of their Left Bank apartment. Marc-Antoine quickly joined the Jacobin Club; Jules followed his lead. Rosalie cautiously observed the events taking place in the capital and struggled to interpret the monumental changes around her. However, in 1792, many things changed for Rosalie. Marc-Antoine returned to Romans to help his sisters with the family estate. Jules left for seven months in London, where he fulfilled quasi-diplomatic responsibilities for the revolutionary government. Rosalie became the family journalist, keeping both men apprised of events. By watching and writing about what was taking place, Rosalie created meaning for herself and constructed a clear political philosophy on the far Left.

This radicalization reached its peak during the Terror. Marc-Antoine had aligned himself with the Mountain while a representative to the Convention. He had voted for the king's execution. At the beginning of the Terror, Jules received a new job as traveling agent for the Committee of Public Safety, and he fulfilled his functions diligently and, occasionally, violently. Rosalie and Marc-Antoine's friendship with the Jacobin leaders deepened during this time. They facilitated Jules's correspondence between the Committee of Public Safety and their son, and they also cared for Maximilien Robespierre when he was ill. It was because of her friendships and her family's political roles that Rosalie embraced the ideology of the Terror. As her family members grew increasingly powerful politically, Rosalie's identity changed considerably. In fact, one of the most radical components of her new political philosophy was her support of feminist principles.

Despite Rosalie's proximity to revolutionary power and her faith in her son and her friends to follow the path of virtue, the violence that accompanied the Terror distressed her. Although her misgivings were necessarily obscured, glimpses of those feelings in her correspondence suggest that she worried about Jules, whose violence and vulnerability to political rivals were growing. This trauma peaked on 9 Thermidor, when Robespierre fell, nearly taking her son with him. Once Rosalie had successfully secured her son's safety after he had spent more than a year in prison, she spoke almost never again about the Revolution or the political world.

In her domestic life, Rosalie still had many topics for epistolary conversation. Jules married in 1801, prompting new conversations on family life and child rearing. While advising the young couple on how to set up their household, manage their money, and raise their children, Rosalie developed a classically bourgeois ethic. She also seemed to embrace the ideology of domesticity. In light of this reality, it is questionable if the Revolution had a lasting impact on Rosalie. However, within her intimate letters and private relationships, Rosalie's politicized identity remained intact, although it was perhaps dormant.

This question of "having" a Revolution is the first of three fundamental questions historians ask about the history of women in the revolutionary period. Analyses of political discourse and laws have shown
that women made few gains in equality.[2] Women's classification as "passive citizens" with limited political roles separated them clearly from
the group of men who were "active citizens." Thus historians discuss
the "limits of citizenship" for French women.[3] They argue that women's
roles in public retracted during the Revolution. Whereas women of the
popular classes had enjoyed a traditional role of speaking against injustice in the Old Regime, in the New Regime political leaders sought to
silence women as a way of controlling the urban crowds. Meanwhile, the
ideal republican woman became modeled on the Roman mother who
"demonstrated her patriotism by staying at home."[4] The Napoleonic
Code eventually subordinated women definitively to their husbands
and fathers.

The second question is how women's subordination to men was integral to the political order of the New Regime.[5] Joan Landes argues influ-
entially that "the bourgeois republic was constituted in and through a
discourse on gender relations."[6] As revolutionaries constructed a new
society, they first confirmed the difference between men and women
and believed that from that natural difference, distinctions in law
should follow. The exclusion of women from politics was therefore
fundamental to the New Regime and impossible to reverse.[7] Others
similarly suggest that revolutionary psychology involved a strong desire
on the part of the male leadership to contain the women who were
potentially liberated after the dissolution of hierarchies.[8] This initial
exclusion of women from the universal ideals of liberty and equality
made discussions of real equality difficult if not impossible for early
feminists.[9]

However, policies and rhetoric are one thing, and women's lived
experience is another. As historians have more recently studied wom-
en's actions and interactions with the legal system during this period
in France, they have realized that the history of women is more
complicated than previously thought. The author of one significant
study asserts that no fundamental exclusion of women buttressed

republicanism. Rather, the family was a crucial site of politicization for men and women alike. Analysis of family courts demonstrates that gender relations were indeed integral to the New Regime, but those relationships became more, not less, egalitarian.[10] An additional study of the family offers evidence complementary to that argument, and surprisingly so, as the researcher looked at the period that most historians consider to be the end of women's opportunity for freedom: the first several decades of the Napoleonic Code. This analysis reveals that contradictory laws related to citizenship and family rights led to ongoing disputes in court. Judges had to reconcile conflicting laws that made women either citizens before wives or the other way around. The presence of these conflicts indicates not only that women made legal gains in relation to their families but also that there was no decisive moment of women's subjugation. The relationships between men, women, and the state were complex, and women's subordination was not inevitable at the outset of the Revolution.[11]

As a result, there is a third question: Given the fact that women's opportunities for political expression were different from men's, how did women participate in the Revolution? The range of political actions in which women from the popular classes engaged has sometimes been defined so broadly as to include subtle actions such as joining uncounted voices in a vote in addition to more visible behavior such as taking part in the violent *journées*, or days of action. Analysis of this group of women, the militant women of the popular classes, can be a guide for studying a different category of women about whom we know even less, the women of the middle class.[12]

Of course, some middle-class women are already well-known. Madame Roland's body of writing has been the subject of several studies.[13] Similarly, Olympe de Gouges's radical *Declaration of the Rights of Woman* has inspired research into her life.[14] As important as these figures were, they were also extraordinary because of their prominence. The dramatic ends of their lives, both under the guillotine in the fall of 1793, further underscore their exceptionality and lend credence to the thesis that the Revolution was hostile to powerful women.

To understand the "majority in their homes," the women who led much more private lives, there are few options. There is some evidence that single or older bourgeois women attended section meetings in Paris, and a handful regularly attended clubs or popular societies.[15] Historians note, however, that those opportunities were short-lived, as women's assembly was banned in 1793.[16] The fact that so little is known about bourgeois women's experiences during the Revolution is vexing in light of the fact that the Revolution is often seen as the turning point in the making of the bourgeoisie.[17] Bourgeois men's common goals for political reform helped form a cohesive social class. One argument states that "political behavior [was] the defining characteristic of the middle classes."[18] Another confirms that the bourgeoisie "considered itself to be a 'new aristocracy' of work, competence, and wealth...and followed an independent and liberal line in politics."[19]

However, these gains benefited men at the expense of women, who were not only denied access to education and positions of author- ity but also distanced from productive labor as business moved out- side the home in the nineteenth century. Furthermore, the ideology of domesticity, which had been gaining momentum since at least the early eighteenth century, became undeniable in the mid-nineteenth century. According to the ideology, a woman's place was within the home, where she perfected her feminine virtues of modesty, sensitiv- ity, chastity, and perhaps some charm. The ascendance of this ideology was directly related to the end of the Revolution, a period of recov- ery when the middle class sought to prove its moral superiority to the classes above and below it, renew social stability through the affirma- tion of class divisions, and bring back a "natural" state of family life that subordinated the wife to the husband.[20] Bourgeois women, then, seem critical actors not only in the Revolution that their husbands led but also in the end of the Revolution, as French men and women sought a return to social stability.

Because very few bourgeois women left records of their experiences of the Revolution, Rosalie's correspondence has tremendous value. The quantity of letters is critical. Nearly every year between 1775 and 1810 is represented, but not with equal distribution. In the Old Regime, a few letters from 1775–1777 and 1779–1784 exist, while there are more from 1785. The first revolutionary letter is dated August 27, 1789. The greatest volume of revolutionary letters comes from the period 1792–1794. In those years, Rosalie wrote nearly twice a week. Her last letter is dated May 28, 1810. In the years after Thermidor, there are more than one hundred letters. This archive allows readers to trace the arc of Rosalie's life and thoughts before, during, and after the Revolution. This fact alone is noteworthy. Rosalie's archive is practically unmatched. Bodies of private, autobiographical writing detailing women's daily lives are extremely few in number, and the expanse of time that Rosalie's correspondence covers is extraordinary.

Just as important is the quality of her letters. Because her correspondents were family members, her letters demonstrate candor and emotion. The letters are also long—at least four large pages each—and eloquent, with elaborate descriptions of her surroundings, events, and feelings. They are filled with quotations from poetry in French and Latin. They reflect the "negligent style" for which female letter writers were praised, which also makes them appear to be true reflections of her thoughts as they occurred to her. An appealing quality of Rosalie's correspondence is the fact that she usually finished her letters moments before sealing and sending them, rarely editing her work.[21] The greatest gifts Rosalie gives the modern reader are her perceptive and vivid descriptions of the public spectacle and the private anguish that formed her revolutionary world.

While Rosalie was never a public figure, the opposite is true of Jules. His tumultuous career did not end after his imprisonment following Thermidor. In prison, he met and befriended Gracchus Babeuf, with whom he collaborated briefly on a journal. After Jules's release from prison, he joined Bonaparte's Army of Italy and worked on a journal in Milan. And then he turned to an old passion of his and his father's, educational reform. He traveled to Switzerland to meet with the educational theorist Johann Heinrich Pestalozzi and intended to bring his principles to France. Jules died in 1848, after witnessing three revolutions and adhering to each successive regime with nearly equal ardor.[22]

It was to Jules that Rosalie wrote most often, and to whom credit for the survival of her letters is due. Jules kept his mother's missives in two chests at the foot of his bed, he reported to her once. At one point he annotated some of them, and he had intended to use them to publish a memoir. Never accomplishing that in his life, he asked his oldest son to do it, but the collection ended up in his daughter's family. That daughter, Stéphanie, had a son named Edouard Lockroy, who was old enough at the dawn of the Third Republic to hope for a political career. He published a small sample of his great-grandmother's letters under the title *Journal d'une bourgeoise pendant la Révolution française*. This volume is not only slim, but it was also edited in order to serve Lockroy's purposes. He had wanted to present himself as the descendant of a patriotic, but not radical, bourgeois republican family.[23]

Lockroy's family later separated the collection of family papers. Some were eventually given to the National Archives in the mid-twentieth century. Others they were convinced to sell, in 1929, to a Bolshevik intellectual who put them into what was eventually called the Institute for Marxism-Leninism. That gentleman was executed in 1938, and for many years, the Jullien archive in Moscow was likely not opened. However, during the Bicentennial of the Revolution, a group of teachers and historians in Romans realized that there had been "a patriot" of some fame from their city. This group, led by Jean Sauvageon, made a microfilm copy of Rosalie's letters in the National Archives, which had not previously been consulted by historians. (In fact, when other historians quote Rosalie, they rely on Lockroy's imperfect publication.) They brought the microfilm to Romans and began the thankless job of transcribing most of the letters. The documents in Moscow later had their moment to reach daylight in 1991. Pierre de Vargas used the opportunity to copy the contents of that file, and Jules's two chests were then reconstituted, in microfilm, in Romans.[24] The Friends of Marc-Antoine and Rosalie Jullien, as the group of Bicentennial researchers called themselves, worked convivially on the Jullien family archive for many years. Their efforts resulted in a locally performed play about Rosalie and Jules, written by Monsieur and Madame Brozille, and the naming of an elementary school, Groupe Scolaire Marc-Antoine et Rosalie Jullien.[25]

Many hands therefore played a part in bringing Rosalie's traces out of the vaults of various archives. Jules and his grandson Edouard had hoped Rosalie's oeuvre would be read by their contemporaries to serve their masculine purposes of fame, honor, and advancement, but today's historians recognize the value of her writing for a different purpose. Rosalie offers answers to many questions in women's history: Did she feel as though she was a meaningful participant in the Revolution? How was her private life affected by revolutions in politics? How did her gender affect her political ideology? Rosalie does not provide insight into all bourgeois women. However, her story helps us understand many of the challenges and changes that middle-class women experienced.[26] The individual's encounter with forces beyond his or her control is the crucible of history. Rosalie's story—her joy, her anguish, her subtle shifts from left to right, her backward glances and hopeful dreams—is integral to the history of revolutionary France.[27]

Rosalie never asked to be famous—in her lifetime or beyond. Her grave sits in a shady corner of the Père Lachaise cemetery, its porous tombstone only years away from being chiseled apart by rain. She could slip away easily into a place beyond our recall. If she is to be so unexpectedly revived, she deserves an honest accounting.

I

The Old Regime

THE SCRATCHING OF quill on paper was a familiar sound to Rosalie. As she sat at her writing desk, the peal of the St. Bernard church bells probably sounded much like music from her native parish, St. Maclou. But St. Maclou's chimes had traveled just a few streets to her home in Pontoise. In her new country residence, the bells of St. Bernard sounded distantly, almost out of earshot, far down a straight dirt road that traversed their small corner of Dauphiné. The silence of the surrounding groves of walnut trees was altogether unusual for this woman born to well-to-do merchants in a town not far from Paris. She thought of that difference and many others when she wrote a letter one afternoon in September 1784. To Louise Dubray, her childhood friend still living in Pontoise, she wrote, "We have established ourselves in M. Jullien's new possessions. I have not left the countryside since May. I am in my little solitary chateau, content like a queen, just as our old oracles predicted."[1] What childhood fantasies had she and Louise shared years ago? What aspirations had the young Rosalie Ducrollay dreamed up as a precocious young girl on the crest of the Enlightenment and the cusp of a new regime?

One thing Rosalie had not expected was to marry. As her allusion to solitude indicates, she thought she would never attract a spouse. She considered herself ugly; her redeeming features were her large, blue-gray eyes. She was also especially well educated and outspoken— unfeminine traits in the eighteenth century. By the time she wrote to Louise, however, she had been married for nearly nine years. She and her husband and their two children had just acquired land near the rest of his inherited property in Dauphiné and were finally able to move out of the home they shared with his mother and two sisters. In many ways, Rosalie lived in a world she probably never imagined as a girl. Surrounded by her husband's family, managing farmland and fulfilling domestic responsibilities, Rosalie experienced many new environments, relationships, and roles after she married.

Rosalie's correspondence begins in 1775, the year she became Marc-Antoine's wife. Her life before marriage is mysterious to some degree, but some things are certain. The first among those is that she received an exceptional education. Although it was not uncommon for a woman in her class and part of the world to be literate, Rosalie's accomplishments far exceeded functional literacy.[2] She probably enjoyed the luxury of private tutors rather than the more typical education for upper-class girls, a two-year stint in a convent. As her good spelling and knowledge of Latin and Italian made her an aberration among even some noblewomen, it is likely that she flourished under tutors' care.[3] Whatever her education, credit is also due to Rosalie's personality, as it is clear she thirsted for knowledge and enjoyed debate.

Her curiosity was precisely what her future husband found most endearing. They seem to have been well matched intellectually, and their courtship developed through their interest in literature and learning. She recollected that in the beginning of their romance, she and Marc-Antoine "delighted in" speaking Italian, which she called "the language of tender souls."[4] She continued to rely on that romantic language, frequently closing her letters, "Adio, t'amo più de mi stesso, mio ben."[5]

While Rosalie was leading a studious life in Pontoise, Marc-Antoine was "chasing his muses," as Rosalie liked to say.[6] Just a year older than Rosalie, Marc-Antoine also shared her appreciation for philosophy. He was the first of six born to a surgeon in Romans, a town in Dauphiné, but he sought the literary circles of larger cities: Grenoble, Lyon, and Paris. Identifying as a "bourgeois," he made his living by tutoring and investing modestly with the help of wealthier friends. His career as a tutor was brief, but he always aspired to be an author, a bona fide *homme de lettres*.

Marc-Antoine's relative proximity to Lyon was useful in his pursuit of literary circles. There he made contact with famous men of letters, especially the abbé Mably, whose writings on equality and virtue were some of the most progressive of the period. According to Rosalie, "The good abbé Mably attached himself to [Marc-Antoine] at first glance."[7] Mably adopted Marc-Antoine as a protégé, investing time and care in his budding career as a philosopher. He also secured Marc-Antoine a lucrative job as a tutor in the mid-1760s, in Paris. Marc-Antoine's charge was a young noble from the very old house of La Rochefoucauld. Mably and Marc-Antoine visited with each other in Paris, and between visits they corresponded. In the philosopher's letters to Marc-Antoine, we see a mentor who cared for his pupil and was not afraid to rebuke him when he went astray.

An instance of discord came shortly after Marc-Antoine moved to Paris, when he began to fall in love. In the capital, he met a young woman from Pontoise—not Rosalie, but Louise Marguerite Metayer, the daughter of a deceased tanner and merchant. He married her in April 1769, and they lived in the home she had inherited in Pontoise. The abbé opposed both the marriage and the couple's decision to move out of Paris. In August 1767, Mably warned Marc-Antoine that marriage would distract him from philosophy and deprive him of a good living as a tutor. Once the marriage was accomplished, Mably wrote sadly: "Your love [for your wife] was stronger than your love for liberty. . . . As much as I had told you to stay free, I now invite you not to struggle in your chains." Although he insisted that he "would love to see" Marc-Antoine back at the La Rochefoucauld home, Mably offered his continued friendship. "I imagine that you will continue to occupy yourself with letters and philosophy; it is a necessity for you. And I invite you to pursue it, both for your happiness and as an honor to philosophy," he wrote.[8] Marc-Antoine took up this invitation and remained in contact with the philosopher through both of his marriages.

Marc-Antoine did continue to dabble in philosophy and reclaim part of his "freedom." His avocation drew him to Paris and away from his wife. Subsequently, he was not at home during two great family tragedies. Louise gave birth to a girl on January 12, 1774, but the baby died the same day. Complications from the birth led to Louise's death ten days later. Marc-Antoine's name is not on either of the death records, but one familiar signature appears: that of Philippe Ducrollay, Rosalie's father.[9]

Rosalie never mentioned her husband's first family in any of her correspondence, although she certainly would have had occasion to meet Louise in Pontoise. In fact, Rosalie and Marc-Antoine's friendship seems to have begun well before Louise died. Rosalie even knew some of Marc-Antoine's family members who lived far away in Dauphiné. She had known Marc-Antoine's youngest sibling, Claire, since her birth in 1762 and remained friends with her throughout Claire's childhood.[10] Similarly, while still newly wed, Rosalie wrote several letters to Marc-Antoine's sister Virginie, who was eleven years his junior. Virginie, too, was already a close friend and confidante.[11] Rosalie and the Jullien girls must have connected in the Julliens' home province when Rosalie was in her twenties. What she was doing in Dauphiné in the 1760s is a mystery.

Even more mysterious are the circumstances of her marriage to Marc-Antoine. The couple claimed they wed in early 1775, about a year after Louise's death. Rosalie and Marc-Antoine's first child, Jules, was born in March 1775. The three of them were living in Paris at the time, and no marriage contract seems to have survived in that city's archive. A historian has indicated that the document is in a Russian archive, and it dates their marriage in 1777.[12] In their writings, however, Marc-Antoine and Rosalie refer to 1775 as the beginning of their marriage. The missing document is not the only problem. Remarkably, despite their cohabitation and their child, they kept their marriage a secret from neighbors, friends, and family for nearly a year. Why?

It is difficult to arrive at an answer because this type of marriage was unusual. Having children out of wedlock was very uncommon for the bourgeoisie.[13] The fact that Rosalie and Marc-Antoine delayed in marrying until just before or after Jules's birth indicates that they did not feel compelled to marry because of the pregnancy.[14] Furthermore, while their conceiving a child six months after Louise's death smacks of poor taste, quick remarriages were not unheard-of in the eighteenth century.

Consequently, Rosalie and Marc-Antoine were likely not silent out of a sense of propriety or respect for the deceased. It is also unlikely that their bashfulness was a result of shame or disappointment about their union, for although it is true that Marc-Antoine valued his independence, this second marriage was undeniably a love match for him and Rosalie.[15]

In the end, the reason behind their unusual choice is unknowable, but it indicates significant defiance in the face of social pressure as well as deep trust in each other to honor their commitment without the oversight of legal, ecclesiastical, or familial authority. Perhaps Rosalie's marriage is one aberration to come out of the widespread changing conception of marriage in the late eighteenth century. This was an epoch when partners assumed greater freedom in their choices and romance replaced pragmatism as the foundation of those choices.[16]

It was apparently Virginie who first knew about the marriage. In the first archived letter from December 1775, Rosalie confided in Virginie, "I live in a space of enchantment among these two objects [Marc-Antoine and Jules] that I adore." She feared that disclosing her marriage would interrupt that peaceful domestic world. She continued: "I am so afraid of change that I oppose your brother's plan to announce our marriage. That would force me to leave my dear retreat, and this idea alone upsets me." Marc-Antoine, however, added in a postscript, "I permit you to tell my secret to Mother as long as she promises to be discreet."[17] Was the secret his marriage or his son, who was already nine months old at the time of the letter? The couple were slow to share the news about both significant events, for whatever reason. The explanation might be as simple as a desire for privacy.

This tendency toward privacy might also explain why Rosalie did not make plans to visit Marc-Antoine's relations in Romans until January 1777. She told Virginie that she was shy about meeting everyone. "It is glorious being the wife of such a man," she began, but she worried that "the opinion that people have about his excellent taste makes them imagine perfection in his choice [of wife]. They think so favorably of me that I dare not show myself in Dauphiné." By then, Rosalie and Marc-Antoine had also disclosed their marriage to their Parisian neighbors and friends, she explained. "I will say happily: my marriage is almost as public here as in Romans." But she confided in Virginie that she did not intend to discuss it much because "I am careful not to expose to the stormy winds of the world a happiness that is almost within their reach."[18] This fear of losing hold of a fragile happiness remained a common refrain throughout her life.

Her fears were justified. In that letter of January 1777, Rosalie also told Virginie that she was pregnant for a second time. She was delighted by "the most beautiful appearance" of her body.[19] She was so happy, in fact, that her contentment evolved into nervousness. She wrote, "Do you know, my dear Virginie, that so much prosperity worries me."[20] Her child, another son, was born later that spring. They named him Bernard, for Marc-Antoine's younger brother. Little Bernard died of smallpox sixteen months later, and Rosalie's fortune turned as she had feared.[21] There are no letters from that time, but Rosalie and Marc-Antoine thought about poor Bernard for the rest of their lives. His memory appears in their letters well into the nineteenth century. He was especially present in Rosalie's mind as she prepared for her third child's arrival. She wrote to her close friend Mademoiselle Tiberge, "My Bernard is still alive in my heart, and the cradle I am preparing for one [child] will often be watered by the tears I shed for the other."[22] Auguste was their third and final child, born in September 1779. He lived a long life, like his brother Jules.

Auguste joined the other three Julliens about a year after they had moved from Paris to Romans. They first took up residence in the Jullien family property, which Marc-Antoine had inherited when his father died in 1775. It included a small house, several acres of walnut trees, and other arable land. The family sold wine, oil, and buckwheat, but the most significant source of income came from leasing out their land to tenant farmers.[23] This type of business generated small but reliable revenue. Leased land and rented homes usually generated a 5 percent annual return on investment. The stability of investing in property drew most prosperous eighteenth-century Frenchmen to that market.[24]

Marc-Antoine and Rosalie's home, Les Délices, still stands in Romans today. The small, square home was Rosalie's retreat during seven years of her sons' childhood, before she spent the majority of her life in Paris. *Photo by author.*

This new rural landscape agreed with Rosalie. She described her surroundings romantically to her husband in the fall of 1785: "I walked around our countryside yesterday with Auguste. Our wheat and our rye cover the earth like a lush carpet that, receiving sunrays through the branches of our majestic walnut trees, form scents so pleasant and fresh that they hint of spring without the flower. When I sense the impressions of these objects winning over my soul, I close my eyes."[25] While she would always be more inclined toward city life, Rosalie relished her retreats to the fresh air and the timeless evolution of bud and flower.

Just as Marc-Antoine had left Romans occasionally as a young man, he continued to make frequent trips to the large cities after moving his small family to the country. Most often, he traveled for business reasons to Lyon, Grenoble, and Paris. Rosalie remained almost constantly in Romans, however, until the family relocated to Paris in December 1785. While in the country for nearly a decade, and often without her husband, Rosalie became a manager of the small estate and caretaker of two children, her ailing mother-in-law, and, to some degree, her young sisters-in-law.

Rosalie's life with her husband's family provides unusual insight into the dynamic among in-laws. Most French couples formed nuclear family households, but Rosalie and Marc-Antoine joined his mother and unmarried sisters in his childhood home. Even when they bought adjoining property with a house they called Les Délices and gained some privacy, they spent significant amounts of time with the Jullien girls. Rosalie got along well with her sisters-in-law. Sometimes she tutored them in reading along with her own sons.[26] Similarly, Rosalie was affectionate with her mother-in-law. When Madame Jullien's declining health made her melancholic, Rosalie wrote with great concern about it to Tiberge.[27] Rosalie expressed affection for and attachment to her husband's mother and siblings. In fact, she seemed more attached to them than to her own relations, including her sister, Charlotte, about whom she never wrote.

The Jullien property was women's domain. With Marc-Antoine often away and his brothers in other cities, the homestead was filled with women. Rosalie and her sisters-in-law managed the land under Rosalie's direction. Despite the fact that Rosalie spent most of her single life in towns, she quickly learned the farm business and helped her family economy grow. One fall day in 1785, she reported to her husband that she went to one of their properties to oversee "the change of the barns and the planting of 40 walnut trees, for which [the peasant] Lombard prepared holes in the *grande allée*."[28] On another occasion, while she was visiting her uncle in Mantes, she wrote to Virginie and instructed her not to sell a mule for less than nine louis. She reminded her that a neighbor "sold his mule for 9½ louis, and it was not worth as much as ours."[29] All of the Jullien women were experienced property managers and practical businesswomen. They acted almost in the absence of men, in an environment that blended the pleasures of the leisure class with the diligence of farmers.[30]

Rosalie was not only savvy but also industrious. In July 1779, she wrote enthusiastically to Tiberge about the lucrative and intellectually stimulating hobby of raising silkworms: "These insects demand a lot of attention, and they give back in proportion to the care you give. [My sisters and I] keep them on tables that occupy large rooms. These tables are a foot long, and in the last period of the insect's life, we make little nests of heather on each of them, and all of the silk-worms hang on one of the branches in their brilliant and rich graves. They are truly golden apples from Hesperides' garden."[31] Rosalie was indeed innovative. Romans had one of the largest concentrations of silk mills in the area—twelve, to be exact—which were placed along the Isère River. But they did not appear until 1787, nearly ten years after Rosalie and her sisters-in-law began raising their worms.[32] Both Rosalie's business sense and her scientific curiosity found satisfaction in this hobby.

The Jullien women ran the farming business, but they were far from the only workers on their land. Rosalie lived among many people, including lease farmers, peasants, and domestic servants. This lifestyle caused her to reflect in February 1782 on how country living was often less tranquil than life in Paris. She wrote to Marc-Antoine, who was in Grenoble: "Oh dear solitude of Paris, how we miss you! By way of an extraordinary contradiction, it is true that [in Paris] we enjoyed a retreat in the middle of many people, but here we have many people in the middle of our retreat."[33]

As the property owner, Rosalie had a good rapport with the many laborers. After visiting two properties that she and Marc-Antoine acquired after 1788, she recounted that "all of the farmers sent me their felicitations and offered their most respectful obedience." The servants' fond respects were also to be passed along to Marc-Antoine: "All of our domestics beg me to name them.... Everyone sends thousands of good wishes."[34] In 1785, Rosalie acquired a domestic servant, Marion, who would become her lifelong companion and friend. She told her husband, "I have a domestic servant who serves me with an affection that leaves me nothing to desire."[35] Marion remained a part of their family at least until the end of Rosalie's correspondence, and probably until the end of her life.[36]

The portrait of Rosalie's family would not be complete without a discussion of their dearest friends. This handful of confidants formed an extended family for Rosalie and Marc-Antoine; they also became useful contacts and hosts in major cities throughout France during the Revolution. One of Rosalie's oldest and dearest friends was Louise Françoise Dubray, née Huppe. Three others were consistently part of her life before, during, and after the Revolution: Madame Nugues, Madame Dejean, and Mademoiselle Tiberge. Charlotte and Claude Nugues lived with the Julliens in Romans, and the families, with children the same ages, were probably each other's best friends. Madame Dejean lived in Versailles and was a close and useful friend during the Revolution. In 1801 Rosalie wrote a poem and dedicated it to Dejean, "my friend for forty years."[37] Mademoiselle Tiberge lived in Paris, in the faubourg Saint-Germain, and seems to have developed a close relationship with Rosalie and Marc-Antoine while they lived in and near Paris before they wed.[38]

Once the Julliens moved to Romans in 1777 or 1778, they continued to nurture their friendship with Tiberge. The method for doing that in the eighteenth century was to write letters, to enter into "commerce" with someone. As Goodman notes, letter writing was "the matrix and the medium in which friendship developed."[39] Friendship was far from casual in Rosalie's day. According to one secrétaire, or letter-writing manual, friendship was "a tender feeling of the soul which leads us to share with someone complete and honest intimacy, stemming from a conformity of thought, opinion, affections, intentions."[40] In a 1751 encyclopedia article on friendship, Denis Diderot and Claude Yvon began by referring to communication, including epistolary communication, explaining that friendship is "the practice of maintaining a decent and pleasant commerce with someone." They went on to liken friendship to virtue. A well-maintained "friendship relieves [virtuous men's] hearts, relaxes and broadens their minds, makes them more confident and lively, enhances their play, work, and mysterious pleasures. It is the soul of their lives as a whole."[41]

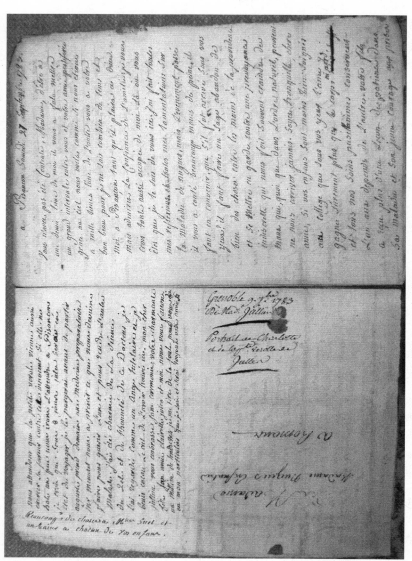

Rosalie liked to fill every inch of paper, which she folded and sealed with wax. She wrote this letter from Grenoble to Charlotte Nugues in Romans to tell her that she had just enjoyed a visit from Saint-Cyr. *Photo by author.*

Friendship was very important to Rosalie. About *amitié* (friendship), she wrote, "It is always my favorite deity, the idol of my heart."[42] Through her dedicated letter writing, we see her worship that deity. She particularly celebrated the idea that friends share a likeness of spirit. After a visit to Tiberge in Paris, Rosalie asked her to reciprocate the visit. "As you have a soul like ours, dear friend, you know exactly how we felt when we saw you." Marc-Antoine wrote a postscript: "I told [Rosalie] that I did not leave Paris and my dear Tiberge without a tug at my heart. It is true, my dear friend, that if it were not for the sweet ties that chain me to my excellent family," he would have stayed in her company.[43]

Just as friends were supposed to be equally obliged to each other, correspondents demanded reciprocity when they expressed affection.[44] Letters between friends often sound to modern ears like love letters. From 1700 to 1770, the following was a common phrase between men: "Love me as well as I do you, and you will love me well indeed."[45] In this emotional epistolary universe, friends could express their demands dramatically. Rosalie wrote several letters to Tiberge expressing her sadness and anxiety over the lack of letters from her. She finished one plaintive letter, "Monsieur Jullien says that if you are not dead, we will kill you." When a letter arrived from Tiberge that same day, Marc-Antoine added a postscript: "[Rosalie] sees that you are alive, but she worries that your friendship is dead in your heart because you were silent for so long."[46] On the other hand, Rosalie explained to friends that she wrote them for no other reason than not to let her correspondence lag.[47]

The Nugues family consisted of Claude and Charlotte (née Enfantin) and their nine children, including Jules's best friend, Saint-Cyr, born in 1774. They were a very wealthy middle-class family, in part because of Claude's career as a lawyer and also because of their lucrative investments. On several occasions, Marc-Antoine helped Claude carry out his business in Lyon and Grenoble. Their wealth dwarfed that of the Julliens. The Nugues *hôtel* in the city center was a prominent home. Their estate in nearby rural Curson was a stately presence in the country. Recently, the impressive Curson home was full of delicate eighteenth-century furnishings that Claude and Charlotte's descendants enjoyed.

The Nugueses and Julliens were very dear friends. Charlotte told Claude in 1784, "Madame Jullien sends you much *amitié* and [offers] help if needed. Truly, my friend, this family seems to love us quite sincerely."[48] There was such love between them that Claude was Auguste's godfather (Virginie was his godmother), and their children grew up almost as brothers. Rosalie enjoyed Charlotte's companionship, especially when they were pregnant at the same time and could help each other prepare for their children.[49] She was similarly fond of Claude, with whom she always "disputed a little," she wrote in a letter to Charlotte. This banter was a good sign of friendship, she added.[50]

The parents also offered each other help and consolation in difficult times. Charlotte confided in Rosalie about how she missed her eldest daughter, also named Charlotte, when the girl was sent to a convent for her education. Claude helped the Julliens run business errands when Marc-Antoine was ill for many weeks in the spring of 1779.[51] Perhaps the most trying times of all were when the Jullien or Nugues children contracted smallpox. Jules suffered from it in the summer of 1780, and Auguste's case was worse in 1783.[52] They also enjoyed many special occasions together. One day in January 1794, Rosalie, Charlotte, and sundry relatives went to see a hot-air balloon. Charlotte described the spectacle: "We went the same day, all together, to the château bleu where the whole city was assembled to see the arrival of a globe...it was rather considerable [in size] but made of thin paper. As soon as it was inflated it went up, making some below laugh and others afraid."[53]

The parents' friendships were strengthened by the affection that their children had for each other. When Saint-Cyr left for boarding school in Paris at age ten and Jules was nine years old, the boys wrote endearing letters to each other. Jules told Saint-Cyr that his distance "saddens and afflicts me, but, my friend, I have to console myself and think about how happy I will be when you return. In the meantime, we must write each other and tell each other everything that we think.

What are you doing in the country? Are you well or ill? Are you having fun, or are you bored? Tell me if you are happy and content, and that will suffice to make me that way, too. I cannot talk for too long with you because I have to learn a verse of Latin. So adieu, my dear friend, I embrace you with all my heart, and I am your best friend for life. Marc-Antoine Jullien."[54]

Saint-Cyr responded: "My dear friend, yesterday morning I received your letter. It gave me an inexpressible pleasure." He offered Jules a description of life at school. They took walks on Wednesdays. They slept in "little alcoves, everybody with his own bed, trunk, and other furniture." They were translating *selecta e profanis scruptoribus historia* and Phedre's fables. They had taken a trip two days earlier to the Château de Vincennes, on the outskirts of Paris, "which I found very large, very old, and very well fortified." Then he wanted to be sure to introduce Jules to his new friend, Mauduit. "My best friend, after my brothers, you, and Bovet, is someone named Mauduit," he reported. "He is the strongest one in our class. I think that when you get here, you will be good friends." Mauduit introduced himself in a postscript: "Monsieur, the great *amitié* that I feel for Monsieur Saint-Cyr as well as the favorable description he has given me of you have led me to write you a note. I would like to ask for a place in your heart...I hope to share with you the most tender *amitié*, if I dare say so." For Saint-Cyr's part, he signed his letter, "Your friend for life."[55] He was only ten years old at the time, but he did not lie. Saint-Cyr's handwriting is mingled with Rosalie's in the letters that Jules saved throughout his life. Once Jules joined Saint-Cyr, he did become friends with Mauduit, whom Rosalie found "very likable."[56]

Although Rosalie maintained many relationships with those nearby and those far from her in Romans, she spent the greatest portion of her time alone with her children. In fact, the Julliens' purpose in living in Romans was not to become prosperous landowners but to raise their children as Jean-Jacques Rousseau suggested, in the country. In this rural environment, they could follow the philosopher's dictates and nurture their children's bodies and spirits. Rosalie reminded Jules when he was a teenager that she and his father had moved to Romans to give him the best possible childhood. "Do you know that since the first moment you were born, we sought to give you a healthy soul and body? Do you know that we lived in the country during your childhood to strengthen your physique?"[57]

From Jules's own descriptions, this bucolic life sounds like a pleasant environment for young boys. Jules and his mother wrote a letter to Tiberge in 1780 to try to convince her to visit Romans from Paris. The five-year-old rallied all of his descriptive powers to entice the friend to their home. "My good friend Tiberge," he wrote, "I beg you to come see us. We are in the country in a charming place. We have superb prairies, we have all sorts of fruits that are excellent. My little brother is very handsome. He knows how to play hide-and-go-seek, my mother hides and he finds her right away. My father is going to Lyon, which makes us very upset because he is a good papa and we love him a lot."[58] Given Jules's age at the time and the fact that his spelling was worse when he was ten years old and away at school, it seems that Jules copied his mother's writing, probably a transcription of Jules's spoken words, in producing this letter.

Because of Marc-Antoine's absences, Rosalie bore most of the parenting responsibilities. She was the one who ensured that the boys practiced reading and writing, as four-year-old Jules explained to his father in September 1779. Jules added a postscript to his mother's letter. It was pedagogically useful that his father was away from home, but Jules was unhappy he was gone. "My dear Papa, I am very upset that you left without saying goodbye." He continued, "I am doing very well [as is] my little brother Auguste. Our garden is full of roses.... Adieu my dear papa. I am writing to win six chestnuts, adieu once more dear papa." Although his chestnut treat encouraged him on, he admitted that he was "weary of writing" because he had also written four friends, including Tiberge, Dejean, and Dubray.[59] The letter-writing practice served two functions for young Jules: it helped his writing skills, and it introduced him to the functions of *amitié*.

Once Jules had grown strong in the country, it was time for him to start formal schooling. Marc-Antoine and Jules moved back to the capital in September 1785 so that he could go to *collège* where his uncle

Bernard was a teacher and where Saint-Cyr was waiting for him. Rosalie followed with Auguste three months later. It was unusual for parents to accompany their children to boarding school. Rosalie explained it was a way of keeping Jules "under our wing."[60] She worried over this big change for Jules. She asked Marc-Antoine when they first arrived how the "little kids from Romans," including Jules and Saint-Cyr, were doing in the big city. "I picture him in his school like a Huron in Paris," she said, fearing the boy from the country would look foreign and uncivilized to his classmates. "My poor Jules, my poor Jules, from here I can see you, awkward and gauche."[61] She was so concerned that she had dreams about Jules arriving at school unprepared, embarrassing himself before the little Parisian pupils. She quoted La Fontaine: "A dream, a nothing, everything worries us when it concerns someone we love."[62]

Rosalie's concern was augmented by the fact that she missed Jules, who had become her closest companion while Marc-Antoine traveled and she and a toddling Auguste lived in Romans. She once explained to Marc-Antoine that Jules, at four and a half years old, was old enough for adult conversations. She and Jules would cry together over Marc-Antoine's absences.[63]

Her fears were quickly calmed, however. Jules was a studious boy. After all, he lived alone with his father, who had been a tutor. Rosalie wrote to Jules with confidence, exclaiming proudly, "I make as much progress in ignorance as you do in science."[64] She wrote him a long letter with many updates from her visits with friends. At the end she wrote, "I talk to you as to a man. Aren't you used to the language of reason? Your heart will make you understand. Weren't you my friend here, my little confidant, my businessman?"[65] Three days later, she wrote to her husband about how proud she was of her "second Emile," referring to Rousseau's educational book by that name.[66] She said Jules had always been a well-behaved child, and now as a pupil at school he was becoming the model citizen that Rousseau had imagined.

This praise for Jules was accompanied by frustration over Auguste, who had been in a bad mood that day. She told Marc-Antoine that his "small disobedience was severely punished with three meals of dry bread—the punishment was multiplied because of his complaints."

Although she was "not happy with him," she was "rather happy with myself" for being firm. She also asked Marc-Antoine to "write him a reproachful letter; that would help me."[67] With her "second Emile" out of the house, Rosalie quickly learned that Auguste had a different temperament. While the family of four always wrote fondly to each other throughout their lives, there were clear differences in their various relationships. The bond between Rosalie and Jules was difficult to improve upon or mimic. Auguste received his mother's punishment rather frequently, perhaps more than he would have if not for the comparison to his brother.

But Auguste also received her care and tutelage. Reading and writing were her primary focus. Rosalie especially encouraged the brothers to write to each other, which they began to do the first fall that Jules was in Paris. Six-year-old Auguste was delighted with Jules's first letter, according to Rosalie's report: "Your little brother was enchanted by your letter. He read it and showed it to anyone who would listen. He gave a silly response. 'I do not have any ideas,' he told me this morning, 'but give me my pretty little letter, I will copy it.' And so, changing the names, he wrote his response here." Auguste's note reads, "Bonjour, my dear Jules, how have you been since I last saw you? Do you go often to the *comédie*? Do you see your friend Saint-Cyr often? Do you still love me?" He named several friends to say hello to and closed, "[M]y dear friend I love you with all my heart. Finished."[68]

Rosalie was gratified when her teaching efforts paid off, especially in Auguste's case. She frequently complained about his lack of concentration, but one day she was able to say, "I am rather happy with Auguste. He is submissive, but he still talks too much. I hope that I am beginning to correct that. Patience and consistency: the two necessary virtues in education and in almost every life circumstance."[69] Rosalie was also consistent with Auguste's reading schedule. She read Homer, Virgil, Fénelon, Rousseau, and La Fontaine with him nightly because she believed that the lessons contained in those readings, if "practiced with austere discipline," would "develop and improve the forces in his soul."[70]

Although Auguste's relationship with his mother was different from that between his mother and Jules, there was still considerable affection between the mother and her younger son. Rosalie wrote to Marc-Antoine one day in the fall of 1785, "Auguste told me yesterday, 'Maman, I would like to have a heart on each side so I could love you with two hearts.'...Don't you admire this little six-year-old boy who talks with the air of Racine? The other day he told me in the same tone: 'How I thank Heaven for giving me a mother like you!'" She also gladly reported that he had sat quietly for two hours while friends visited. "I won't shout 'victory,' but I will record the score."[71]

Rosalie and Marc-Antoine put considerable thought into how to cultivate a close, supportive family. One key to that environment was to foster feelings of equality rather than strict hierarchy. Ideas about marriage and the family were revised throughout the eighteenth century. For centuries, secular and religious authorities had filled the family unit with symbolic importance, recognizing it as a stabilizing force in society and a microcosm of the state. The family's head, the husband and father, had absolute authority over the dependents in the household just as the king had absolute authority over his subjects. The Church similarly supported a strong male head of household, citing especially Saint Paul, who explained that wives should submit to their husbands' leadership. In the eighteenth century, however, the Church began to change its model of marital relations. As Flandrin notes, whereas earlier the husband was responsible for the spiritual well-being of his wife, in the eighteenth century, "the Church counted on the wife to improve her husband" through her inspirational virtue.[72] This shift accompanied a trend in literature, most eloquently expressed by Rousseau, that celebrated companionship between spouses.[73]

A companionate marriage was the goal for many eighteenth-century couples, particularly in the middle class. Another future revolutionary, Manon Roland (née Phlipon), hoped to find a spouse with whom to form a Rousseauian family. She sought a soul mate and feared that "the encounter of two souls that resemble each other, of two lovers united by virtue [was] the winning ticket of the lottery of happiness that is drawn scarcely once a century."[74] In very similar language, Rosalie wrote about winning such a lottery. She told Marc-Antoine that her love was "so extraordinary, so excessive, so tender, so true, so perfect, so perfectly all that it should be, that it merits all of your soul's attention and all of your heart's gratitude."[75]

This companionship and affection belonged not only to spouses but also to parents and children. In *Emile*, Rousseau advised fathers not to punish their children for fear they would become too submissive in adulthood. Rosalie claimed that she and Marc-Antoine followed this advice when she told Jules later in life that they never issued "a reproach, a complaint, or the tiniest punishment." Instead, "*amitié* and esteem" flowed from "the most excellent of fathers and the most sensitive of mothers."[76] (Considering Auguste's dry-bread punishment, this memory might be a little fictional, but Rosalie certainly liked the idea of a conflict-free childhood for her sons.) The Church similarly promoted friendly relations between parents and children, claiming, "Children must 'love their father and mother,' 'having for them a heartfelt affection, giving them proof of it on the appropriate occasions.'"[77] The triumph of paternalism over patriarchy is apparent in many places. One study found that "filial love, parental love, and conjugal love are all included in the single rubric of 'friendship.'"[78] In fact, parents and children addressed each other differently in their letters over the course of the century. After 1770, a common closing was, "I love you and embrace you with all my heart and soul, I am your father and your friend."[79]

Rosalie and Marc-Antoine were individuals drawn to each other because of their similar intellectual capacities, and they entered their marriage thoughtfully as companions. They saw parenthood as a vocation that required diligence, thoughtfulness, and a great deal of love. Whether their home was always the paradise they described in writing is questionable, but their desire to create a romantic image was plain. In reality, trying to raise children in an increasingly competitive world while running a family business and caring for numerous old and young extended family members was hard work. Rosalie's experience in the country was a formative one. She developed practical business skills, self-reliance, and an understanding of the local economy; she embraced innovations and progress; and she caught on to the rhythm of the countryside and was comforted by its eternal meter.

It is not surprising, then, that Rosalie wrote so contentedly to Madame Dubray from her "solitary chateau" when she and Marc-Antoine moved into Les Délices. The house was modest, but it was a place to raise children in the robust country air, and it was a home where a nuclear family could pursue a philosophical existence, steeped in sentimentalism but structured by responsibilities. "Aux Délices," Rosalie established a new and pleasant routine. She described her typical day to her husband in October 1785: "I go to Mass at eight o'clock, and then I have lunch, my sisters say hello, and I get back to business. I work, I write, I read."[80] Simply stated, this explanation of her life is nonetheless thorough. Rosalie thought of herself chiefly as a member of a family, a religious person, a landowner, and an intellectual.

2

Reading for Revolution

WHEN ROSALIE PACKED up to leave Romans for Paris in December 1785, she was careful about the family's great collection of texts. "Our books embarrass us. They are the possessions that I love the most," she told her husband.[1] Over the next several decades, those books made many trips among Rosalie, Marc-Antoine, and their two sons. The well-worn pages and smoothed leather bindings kept them company, comforting them as friends would in unfamiliar circumstances. In some cases, the authors themselves had been real friends of the Julliens.

Aloof from and not very interested in the details of farm business, Marc-Antoine lived in the world of ideas. He had measurable success at joining the Republic of Letters, at least in terms of the friendships he made. One important friend was Joseph Michel Antoine Servan, a native of Romans, an *avocat général* of Grenoble, and man of letters, who, along with his brother, remained a lifelong friend of the Julliens. Servan was also an acquaintance of Voltaire, critical of religious intolerance, and an author of essays that exposed the injustices of the criminal system under the Old Regime.[2]

In the 1780s, Servan turned to Rousseau. He spoke in Lyon about the "citizen from Geneva" in 1781. He was probably rehearsing the ideas that would go into *Reflections on the Confessions of J. J. Rousseau*, which he published in 1783. Rousseau had died in 1778. Servan had met the philosopher and admired much of his work. But, as he explained in his *Reflections*, he also found fault with Rousseau. The philosopher "wanted to bring light," but instead he "lit a fire," Servan claimed.[3] He wrote similar ideas to Marc-Antoine in 1781, in a letter suggesting that Rousseau's fans were too exuberant. Marc-Antoine replied, "Terrible man for wanting to take away my enthusiasm for Rousseau!...Do not hope for it, do not desire it, because you can no more weaken my veneration for this great man than you can weaken my veneration for virtue."[4] He then responded with "cold analysis" to the points in his friend's argument. In the process, he showed himself to be a well-read and intellectual man who was equally aware of Rousseau's romantic novels and his political essays. Marc-Antoine was not just a fan; he was an informed enthusiast.[5]

Rosalie also read widely. In her letters, she referenced translated works from England, Spain, and Ireland. She read poetry, plays, novels, and nonfiction. She quoted Racine, Molière, and La Fontaine more often than she did Voltaire or Montesquieu. She loved history, Eastern philosophies, and works of science.[6] Of course, Rosalie could not avoid Rousseau in her home, but her "enthusiasm" for his work was weaker than that of her husband. On the other hand, religious faith was more important to her than it was to Marc-Antoine. A variety of ideologies formed Rosalie's worldview on the eve of the Revolution.

Rosalie was not only surrounded by philosophical books; she also lived with a philosopher. Marc-Antoine and Servan had written to each other since at least 1776, and probably much earlier, because the letters from that year reveal an old friendship. In a letter of condolence, probably on the occasion of Marc-Antoine's father's death, Servan exclaimed, "Without doubt, it is lucky to be loved by a heart like yours! And how it is sweet to be able to console it!"[7] They continued to write each other while Servan traveled to Lausanne, Switzerland, in 1782. From there, Servan reported on international politics, including the young United States.[8] Servan had likely met Rosalie at least once, when he visited in the summer of 1781. He congratulated Marc-Antoine on his "domestic happiness" at that time. "Your soul seems to me truly delighted by it, and I have never known anyone who adored his domestic gods with as much devotion as you."[9]

Although Servan judged that he was "unworthy" of such domestic relationships, he was an affectionate friend. He opened his letters to Marc-Antoine, "My dear and estimable compatriot," and he closed them, "Adieu my dear compatriot, I kiss you cordially."[10] A scholar by nature, he wrote thoughtfully about their friendship. "Tell me your thoughts on my ideas.... My heart has a thousand ears for yours. Tell me everything, and I will respond frankly. In friendship, that goes without saying. I am very attached to you, and for a long time; and that is a singular thing."[11] In another instance, he asked Marc-Antoine jovially to "think of me often, love me always, and tell me so sometimes."[12] As noted previously, friendship was taken seriously in the eighteenth century, and maintaining an active correspondence was critical to the quality of a friendship.

Within this context, it is clear that Marc-Antoine's long defense of Rousseau was sent in the spirit of friendship and intellectual discourse. In a six-page letter to Servan, Marc-Antoine opened with warm greetings of *amitié*, followed by a challenge: "[I]t is impossible to weaken my veneration for this *grand homme*.... Let us enter into details."[13] Marc-Antoine discussed the nature of man and society, theater and music, popular sovereignty, education, and virtue. He cited Rousseau, referencing *The Social Contract*, *Emile*, and *The New Heloise*, with direct paragraph citations.

He believed, like Rousseau, that men were born good. Citing *The Social Contract*, he asserted that society was corrupted because of bad government. But he assured Servan that "Rousseau absolutely thinks that society would be good if governments were good. Read the beginning of the eighth chapter of the first book of the Social Contract, and the last paragraph of the fourth chapter of the second book."[14] In those passages, Rousseau wrote that when man leaves nature, "his faculties are so stimulated and developed, his ideas so extended, his feelings so ennobled, and his whole soul so uplifted" that he transforms from "a stupid and unimaginative animal" into "an intelligent being and a man." In the second passage Marc-Antoine cited, Rousseau wrote that leaving nature gives men a "better and more secure" way of life, where "instead of natural independence they have got liberty...a right which social union makes invincible." Marc-Antoine then concluded, "If in a moment of black humor he sent the sage into the woods, it was only because he saw more ferocious beasts in the cities." Marc-Antoine also supported direct, popular sovereignty as the only way to avoid "slavery."

But his greatest compliment was for *Emile*, "of all the books I know, the one that speaks the most powerfully to my heart." Marc-Antoine and Rosalie followed some of Rousseau's guidelines for raising children, but Marc-Antoine told Servan that *Emile* was not only useful for "forming children." It was also "excellent for reforming men." He praised Rousseau for showing readers "that it is a sacred duty for a mother to nourish her children, a duty for the father to raise them." This duty, as Marc-Antoine well knew, was political as much as it was familial. In order for Rousseau's social contract to work, children had to develop both their reason and their sentiments. Only reasoning, feeling, virtuous citizens could overcome personal interest and commit themselves to the general will and the common good. Rousseau's emphasis on virtue inspired great respect in Marc-Antoine, who passionately attested, "Jean-Jacques alone knew how to persuade us. Sensitive hearts opened easily to the sweet warmth of his eloquence; rocks were broken under the strike of his brilliant lightning. What virtue did he omit to preach? Or what virtue did he preach without effect?"

For *The New Heloise* he had similar praise. At first he agreed with Servan that it could be "dangerous for a young person who was well-born" to read the romantic novel. "I would not read it to my daughter while she was a girl," he admitted. Instead, he "would reserve it as the most beautiful wedding present that she could receive from my hand." As for himself, "I will read this charming book unto the end of my life, and I will never read it without shedding the sweetest tears, without wanting to be the best husband, best father, and best friend." This emotional response to Rousseau is very similar to that revealed in letters from another fan, a bourgeois named Jean Ranson. Ranson wrote, "Everything that l'Ami Jean-Jacques has written about the duties of husbands and wives, of mothers and fathers, has had a profound effect on me."[15] Like many, however, Ranson was impressed by the sentimental writing Rousseau produced. Marc-Antoine engaged Rousseau's political philosophy *and* sobbed over his romantic novels.

The other distinguished author with whom Marc-Antoine corresponded was Mably. This philosopher was also dear to Rosalie, who met "the good abbé" several times. Mably had not supported Marc-Antoine's decision to marry his first wife. When he met Rosalie, however, their encounter went well. In March 1776, about a year into their marriage, the couple and baby Jules received a visit from the philosopher in Paris. They returned the visit often, Rosalie recalled in a letter to Jules from 1792: "Twenty years of a deepening acquaintanceship [between Marc-Antoine and Mably] fortified their mutual esteem, and we so cherished this philosopher that we visited him often. I, unworthy, passed long evenings with him, little Jules on a seat near me, and your brother in my arms. He caressed you with interest, and said I was a good mother. He had an apparent coolness that gave him a great air of dignity."[16] Apparently Rosalie and the children had won over the philosopher who eschewed family life. Mably's approval surely gratified Marc-Antoine.

Later, Mably would be quoted often by revolutionaries and by Rosalie—much more so than Rousseau, in the latter case. Through letters and during visits, Mably and the Julliens must have discussed his political ideas. Keith Baker has called Mably's writings a "script for a French Revolution."[17] In Mably's view, France had been perpetually unstable politically, undergoing constant revolutions, because it had no fundamental laws, no germ of a constitution. In 1758, he wrote *The Rights and Duties of the Citizen*, which was published in 1789. In it, Mably described the power struggles that were then taking place between the crown and the *parlements*, or courts of law.[18] He believed that these conflicts should evolve into a revolution that would bring about France's first legitimate government. *The Rights and Duties of the Citizen* was written as a dialogue in which an English Commonwealth man, Lord Stanhope, expounded on the virtues of constitutional government. Stanhope argued in favor of limiting the power of the king and separating legislative and executive branches. Like Rousseau, Mably placed sovereignty in the people. Mably therefore suggested a *révolution ménagée* (controlled revolution), begun by magistrates in the *parlements*, who would lead the Third Estate to overthrow the regime.[19]

Probably even more influential than his political philosophy were Mably's views on wealth and poverty. One of Mably's most extreme stances was his opposition to private property. In *The Rights and Duties*, Mably imagined a desert island where all were "equal, all rich, all poor, all free, all brothers, [and] our first law would be to possess nothing as private property."[20] His compassion for the poor also came across in his personal writing to Marc-Antoine. In 1768, Mably wrote him a scolding letter about how he had abused the servants in the La Rochefoucauld house:

> Why do you put on airs with the domestics at the *hôtel*? It is so easy to be kind to people of this station. When one maintains the principles of equality according to the principles of morality and philosophy, one begins to regard inferiors as equals. One does not become them, but one loves them. It is unjust not to be indulgent toward others when one needs so much indulgence from everyone else. Voilà the condition of men: they must support each other mutually, and not to see that is to be prideful or blind.... To put it another way, we must be in perpetual negotiation with men, ceding some things and gaining others.[21]

This rebuke seems to have had an effect on Marc-Antoine, because Rosalie regularly praised him for his fairness toward and compassion for the lower classes.

Marc-Antoine's enthusiasm for Rousseau and Mably surely prepared a political mind-set that became relevant during the Revolution. It was these two philosophers who historians believe were the most influential in forming political ideology in the Revolution. Although Mably's name rarely appeared in National Assembly debates, authors in 1789 and beyond claimed that Mably was one of the most influential thinkers on the topic of liberty.[22] Through his personal relationships and his close reading of political theory, Marc-Antoine was well educated when the Revolution began, well prepared to interpret the change that was under way, and ready to embrace a new order. Rosalie, meanwhile, had learned how to be married to a man steeped in these ideas, to suffer his contemplations, to sanction his frenzy, and to engage his opinions in conversation and debate. Her own philosophy and literary preferences were a little different.

Rosalie called herself a "*sensible*" person, but she rarely wrote about the reigning sentimentalist. She read *Emile* with Marc-Antoine, and she praised Rousseau's descriptive capabilities. When she wrote about Rousseau to her husband, she called him "our friend, Jean-Jacques." But it seems that her husband's enthusiasm for Rousseau grated on her once in a while. In December 1785, for example, she wrote to him, "*Tais-toi* [shut up], Jean-Jacques!"[23] He had wanted to rethink a portion of their plan for the boys' education, and Rosalie, apparently, did not.

Whether enamored or not, most women in Rosalie's position would have been at least somewhat affected by Rousseau's revisions of family life. In *Emile*, Rosalie read about the "natural" roles for mothers and fathers; mothers were meant to nurse their children, fathers to be their tutors. With each parent and child filling a different but complementary role in the family, the family unit was to be a virtuous and happy place from which good citizens would emerge and form a society. In this way, women became ever so slightly political as they devoted themselves to Republican Motherhood.

The mother's role in this paradigm was indeed fundamental to the entire political process. Rousseau explained, "We begin to learn when we begin to live; our education begins with ourselves, [and] our first teacher is our nurse."[24] Maternal nursing, rather than wet-nursing, was therefore also politically necessary. Rousseau believed that "the *only* binding natural attachment of one human being to another" in the state of nature was between mother and child. The reason for this was that the nursing child relieved the mother's breasts, and the mother alleviated the child's hunger.[25] The virtuous, nursing mother also helped establish the first social relationship, that between father and child. In addition, because of nursing, women were vulnerable, and they relied on men to be their providers and protectors. The practice of nursing created multiple family ties.

A state composed of these types of families would undergo a revolution in morals, Rousseau believed. In *Emile*, Rousseau explained:

> But when mothers deign to nurse their own children, then will be a reform in morals; natural feeling will revive in every heart; there will be no lack of citizens for the state; this first step by itself will restore mutual affection. The charms of home are the best antidote to vice. The noisy play of children, which we thought so trying, becomes a delight; mother and father rely more on each other and grow dearer to one another; the marriage tie is strengthened. In the cheerful home life the mother finds her sweetest duties and the father his pleasantest recreation. Thus the cure of this one evil would work a wide-spread reformation; nature would regain her rights. When women become good mothers, men will be good husbands and fathers.[26]

Like others in the eighteenth century, Rousseau disparaged the wide-spread phenomenon of wet-nursing, the practice of placing a child with a woman other than the mother for breast-feeding and child care for about the first two years of the child's life. The practice was becoming less common in other European countries, but in France it had grown among the middle and artisan classes. Different groups had different reasons for seeking this form of child care. The more elite families were probably concerned about the toll that breast-feeding was said to take on the mother's health and figure, as well as the prohibition on intercourse during lactation. For the artisans, wet-nursing allowed the mother to continue her productive labor. Her earnings exceeded the cost of the nurse and were necessary to the family budget. The majority of parents who hired wet nurses sent their children to the countryside to live with peasant women. In the 1730s, about half of Parisian babies were sent away.[27]

Rousseau was not alone in condemning this popular decision. The state was deeply concerned with what it perceived to be a declining population, a sign of the country's weakness.[28] Officials connected the imagined decline to wet-nursing. In fact, in the late eighteenth century, the population with the lowest mortality rate (18 to 20 percent) was infants who were nursed by their mothers. Babies who lived with rural nurses had a 25 to 40 percent mortality rate. The highest rate by far, however, was among foundlings, who had a staggering 65 to 90 percent mortality rate.[29] A doctor who was very concerned about this trend is even responsible for the term *mammal*. In 1788, Carolus Linnaeus used the word *Mammalia* to classify the group of animals that nursed their young. While he mostly recycled Aristotle's terms for the other classes, he chose to focus on this rather surprising characteristic for mammals. Only half of mammals, females, have functioning mammae. Alternative labels might have come from more universal qualities, such as hairiness. Linnaeus hoped to valorize maternal feeding as *the* essential quality that distinguished mammals from others in pursuit of changing popular habits.[30]

While Rosalie did not always agree with Rousseau, she did feel strongly about maternal nursing. Once, she wrote to sixteen-year-old Jules about the regrettable practice of wet-nursing: "Do you know that other parents give their children to strangers [to nurse]?"[31] He should be thankful that his parents were not like them, she wrote. When she was pregnant with Bernard, she wrote to Virginie, "As you guessed, I will nurse," and it will be a "pleasure."[32] She continued in a separate letter, "[M]y pregnant belly has the most beautiful appearance"; she would "carry it with honor" and later "take the greatest joy from nursing." She finished, "I am preparing my small affairs with exquisite maternal pleasure, which brings me a thousand happinesses."[33]

Rosalie nursed all three of her children. In fact, when she had to suspend nursing Auguste in February 1781, she was very sad. She and Auguste had both caught a fever. While she convalesced, with "the most tender regrets," she "prepared [herself] internally to quit [her] post" as his nurse.[34] This emotional response to separating herself from her sick child was hardly political. She was not concerned that stopping nursing would lessen the moral development of her young citizen-in-training. But the decision to nurse in the first place was likely one that Rousseau had inspired in the young couple who reread *Emile* so many times. Her description of nursing as her "post" also suggests that she saw it as a social responsibility, not only a familial one.

In some ways, Rousseau's glorification of motherhood was empowering for women. His model made women fundamental to a well-run society. They were at the center of the family, which was to be "a nursery for good citizens."[35] This new discourse had an effect on motherhood in husbands' and wives' missives. Another eighteenth-century couple, Sophie and Bernard de Bonnard, wrote to each other about raising their son. Like Rosalie and Marc-Antoine, the Bonnards read *Emile* dutifully. It is no surprise, then, that Bernard wrote to Sophie, "Breathe this into his gentle and tender soul, inspire our dear son with your *sensibilité*; let us love him for himself, let us not spoil him, let us make him a good man."[36] Rosalie and Marc-Antoine had similar aspirations.

Like Sophie and Bernard, Rosalie and Marc-Antoine enjoyed writing in Rousseau's language about their family happiness. Throughout their first several years of marriage, Rosalie wrote about "this burning tenderness unknown to so many hearts and so well known to ours."[37] On their tenth anniversary in 1785, Rosalie recalled, "I have the most tender love for you, after ten years, the most tender love. I have the most sincere veneration because of my understanding of your soul. I have the most ardent gratitude for the happiness I owe to you."[38] They promoted the qualities that defined the new marriage of the eighteenth century: companionship, romance, and respect.

Companionship was not the same as equality, but Rousseau did advance the idea of complementarity. In a complementary relationship, each role is necessary because it is different from the other. Inherent in that difference is hierarchy. In an often-quoted paragraph, Rousseau explains that "woman is specially made for man's delight." He reaches this conclusion after describing the differences between men and women: "In the union of the sexes each alike contributes to the common end, but in different ways. From this diversity springs the first difference which may be observed between man and woman in their moral relations. The man should be strong and active; the woman should be weak and passive; the one must have both the power and the will; it is enough that the other should offer little resistance."[39] Rousseau's depiction of feminine virtue consisted of meekness, humility, simplicity, timidity, chastity, and submissiveness to the husband.[40]

Thus devoted reader of Rousseau and future revolutionary Manon Phlipon sought a husband to whom she would be happy to subordinate herself. She did tell her friend, however, that she found the female sex's dependence "hateful."[41] Rosalie also saw Marc-Antoine as the head of the household. For example, when she wrote to him about a financial transaction in October 1785, she assured him, "My friend, I will only do what you judge to be good, and so I await your opinion before I respond [to the offer].... When one has an enlightened friend, he must direct everything and hold the reins."[42] Similarly, in a letter to her friend Madame Dejean she explained that she did not to feel equal to her husband in intellect or virtue, but her subordination made her happy.[43] However, it is equally clear from Rosalie's writing that this lip service to patriarchy was far more rhetorical than realistic. Rosalie was aware of the unfairness of Rousseau's image of femininity, and she resisted it.

In fact, the Julliens' marriage was more egalitarian than Rosalie's odes to patriarchal authority would suggest. In truth, her deference to Marc-Antoine's "enlightened" opinion was usually answered with little if any input. Marc-Antoine believed in his wife's abilities to manage the home, finances, and children, as his long absences testify. Even when he was at home, he was not interested in authority. Rosalie complained to Tiberge, "One day I seriously offered [Marc-Antoine] 25 louis to watch his children, but he objected, saying he had too much business to do, adding it was a shame he could not do two things at once."[44] She frequently complained to Marc-Antoine that he was absent too often from their home, experiencing freedom from domestic responsibilities in ways that she was unable to enjoy.

Rosalie preferred Samuel Richardson's models for female virtue. Richardson's romantic epistolary novels were translated from English into French in the mid-eighteenth century. Rosalie read them in the 1780s with her sisters-in-law. In the fall of 1785, the women read *Pamela* and *Clarissa*, two epistolary novels about women who guard their chastity and virtue despite men's attempts to corrupt them.[45] Rosalie wrote to Marc-Antoine about the struggle between Clarissa and Robert Lovelace: "This story charmed us with its variety of characters so well supported, by the insight one gains in the letters of this naughty Lovelace, and finally by the wisdom and the unhappiness [of Clarissa, who is] the model of our sex."[46] Clarissa, the tragic heroine, conformed to the feminine ideals of the period, including chastity and obedience.[47]

Richardson's epistolary novels opened a "new field of pleasure" for the already sentimental Rosalie and shaped the way she wrote about romance, marriage, femininity, and masculinity.[48] In letters to Tiberge, she called Marc-Antoine "Sir Charles Grandison," a name "which contains so much meaning."[49] Charles Grandison was the title character of another Richardson novel. Grandison was meant to be the model of a virtuous man, a defender of female virtue, and the opposite of Lovelace. Rosalie praised her husband's virtue often. In Rosalie's time, masculine virtue combined the image of the classical republican who put the welfare of others before his self-interest with that of a feeling and honest husband and father. Rosalie wrote often about Marc-Antoine's rationality, his fairness, and his commitment to his children.

She told her best friend, Louise Dubray, her reasons for loving her husband. She appreciated "his profound sensitivity, inalterable sweetness, extreme *délicatesse*, goodness, indulgence, elevated soul worthy of Ancient Rome, severe integrity, charm, simplicity, gaiety, and everything that could enter into the composition of the best and most perfect of human beings."[50] To Marc-Antoine, she wrote about their companionship and how his virtue attracted her to him as a friend. In the fall of 1785, she wrote, "I thank Heaven everyday and every moment to have married my soul to a soul like yours. I am proud of this alliance as if it was given to me from what? From the ranks of angels."[51] Rosalie wrote about her husband in many ways, sometimes striking a patriarchal chord but more often describing an emotional, rather more equal, "alliance." Her language was operatic, but the life of her marriage was in fact long and vital despite occasional disagreements.

Richardson gave Rosalie models for virtuous adult men and women, but when she taught her children, she relied on La Fontaine. His simple wisdom, his caring sensitivity, and the vividness of his poetry appealed to Rosalie as an adult as well. As she wrote in 1791, "I add him to all of my sauces because he seasons everything."[52] The lessons Rosalie treasured from La Fontaine were those that emphasized kindness and compassion toward others. As in many other cases, her references to La Fontaine would emerge most frequently during the Revolution, as Rosalie wrote to Jules about how to be a good citizen.

There was another significant source of knowledge from which Rosalie formed her moral outlook and worldview. In an age of increasing secularization and rising anticlericalism, Rosalie was a faithful believer in God and an admirer of religious men. Rosalie believed that faith in God was essential to living a virtuous life. While in Romans, Rosalie went to Mass daily.[53] She once reminded Jules, away at school, "Take care, dear Jules, to do all that you are obliged to do for the Supreme Being, in gratitude for being given your life, your good parents, and so many favors. Pray and love God with all the might of your young heart. Be pious and reverential in your devotional exercises."[54]

This reminder was likely not one Jules received from his father. In October 1785, Rosalie devoted several pages to rebuking Marc-Antoine for abandoning religion. She reasoned with him, "You have an excellent soul; you follow your principles with moral austerity....You have the virtues of a perfect Christian. One single thing is missing."[55] The missing virtue was belief in the Christian god, an error that she warned was unforgivable. In her effort to persuade Marc-Antoine to recover his faith, she first reminded him of their courtship, when they read the lives of saints together. "Remember, my good friend, how we used to admire ecclesiastical history....I saw you touched to the brink of tears by the virtue it had inspired in [the Church's] first believers." Then she recruited Rousseau to strengthen her argument: "[Jesus] is so above humanity that our good Rousseau said, if the death of Socrates was that of a man, then the death of Jesus Christ was that of a god."[56] This letter was her only lengthy defense of Christianity. Either Marc-Antoine repented or they agreed to disagree.

In contrast to Rosalie's multiple expressions of religious belief, she showed no sign, in the Old Regime, of anticlericalism. In fact, she had good relationships with religious men, including one monk who heroically saved Romans from a fire in October 1785. She described the event to Marc-Antoine: "At seven at night all of the bells in the city rang. A violent fire was overtaking a house.... we thought it would soon take over all the corners of the city." They had trouble getting water to the house because it was near the town square, up a steep hill from the river. The fire continued until midnight. Women and children found refuge in the St. Bernard church. Men from the neighboring town helped "bravely." But the hero of the day was a monk. "A legendary Capucin climbed up with a hatchet and attacked the two houses that were on fire, separating them from the ones that touched them. By making this space, he contained the fire and cried with a heroic voice that it would not go any further." If he had not done this, the Nugues *hôtel* would have also burned down. The monk's actions helped ensure that no one was killed.[57]

Religious beliefs joined philosophy in Rosalie's critique of wealth. Wealth bred "pride, selfishness, vanity," the "three tyrants that have exercised their power over [all the world] since the Earth was created, and which reason has combated strongly but in vain since the same date, without ever winning."[58] She feared that wealth had the ability to corrupt even her dearest friends. She called the Nugues *hôtel* a "gilded Palace" and added, "I do not know if that is good."[59] After all, "Happiness and Wealth do not always live in the same house."[60] The *hôtel* was impressive, as were the Nugueses' parties. Rosalie told Tiberge, "If you admire the contemplative and peaceful life, do not look for it among our Epicureans from Dauphiné. They are always with bowl or cup in hand.... Their divine life is the most sensual, mortal life it could be, and the *luxe* at the table is taken to such an extreme that the slightest meal for our petits bourgeois [in Romans] is equal that of your great financiers [in Paris]."[61] Her sensible nature balked at excess.

Rosalie's identity as a member of the bourgeoisie is a final essential part of her worldview before the Revolution. The "great financiers" she mentioned were not modest investors like her and Marc-Antoine; they were a growing political force in the eighteenth century. John Shovlin, in his study of the critique on luxury in the eighteenth century, explains, "By the 1740s, a dense network of marriage alliances linked financiers

An impressive wooden door conceals the corridor leading to the Nugues *hôtel* in the heart of the Romans town center. A plaque informs tourists that Joseph Servan and Saint-Cyr Nugues both occupied the home. *Photo by author.*

with the court aristocracy, giving their children access to the highest offices in the land."[62] When Madame de Pompadour, the daughter of a financier, became royal mistress to Louis XV, the integration of financial and courtly elites was patently clear.

Criticism of the powerful financiers came from many corners, including from Rousseau. In *Discourse on the Sciences and the Arts*, he submitted that attachment to luxury corrupted men and led to despotism. Other critics included people like Rosalie. Members of the "middling elite," including landowners and professionals, were receptive to the philosophers' attack on luxury. Noble and nonnoble elites distinguished themselves from the corrupt financiers by living "according to an ethic of economic discipline and antipathy to frivolous expenditure."[63] The Lamothe family, another eighteenth-century bourgeois family, developed a professional identity and a "service identity" typical of their milieu. Their hard work and morality were displayed through their commitment to the common good. The aristocracy's honor, on the other hand, came from splendor and wealth. Coincidentally, the Lamothe family also "retained a strong emphasis on piety and devotion in their religious lives."[64]

Rosalie fits into this cohort easily. She had a strong sense of identity as an industrious bourgeoise. She told her husband proudly, "Advantages of fortune seem to me so miserable in comparison with the real riches [of virtue]" that they had bred in their children.[65] Rosalie also distinguished this "real" wealth from aristocratic privilege when she wrote about how to merit a title. While Jules was attending school in Paris, she wrote to him, "Our friends, your aunts, your uncle, our servants, our domestic, our farmhands, all call you Jules the Good. That is the surname you must always merit. It is the most flattering and likable of titles."[66]

Her description of her family as modest and virtuous is particularly meaningful as she wrote about it just moments before the Revolution. As a middle-class mother of boys, she particularly bemoaned the inequality of French society. In 1785, she regretted how little impact her sons could have on their peers because of the restrictions they faced as members of the Third Estate. She wrote to her husband, "Because of their birth and fortune, our children are placed in a class of men that can do neither much good nor much bad. If we raise them to be virtuous, it is to make them happy." This reward was significant, and yet Rosalie saw injustice in their situation. She continued: "But these people whom fortune has capriciously placed so high above others, they have such a tremendous influence over those around them that the goodness of one benefits a thousand."[67] Rosalie's awareness of her social position, and the middle-class values she nurtured as a result, was political in a very real sense.[68] How happy Rosalie would become when she saw the Revolution ushering in a period when, in her estimation, virtue was more powerful than wealth, and status was measured by the purity of the soul.

Historians debate the role that ideas played in starting the Revolution.[69] Marc-Antoine was a well-read Enlightenment thinker. His belief in Rousseau's and Mably's political ideologies made him a strong candidate to become a revolutionary. His life seems to lend support perfectly to the theory that ideas make revolutions. Not only was he very knowledgeable about two of the most radical political writers in his lifetime, but he was also similar, to some degree, to the "Grub Street" authors who might have been the conduits through which Enlightenment values became revolutionary actions. These men wanted to become philosophers, but they were constantly frustrated by their inability to gain the status of *philosophes* who were, after all, beneficiaries of government pensions or aristocrats' patronage—that is, part of the existing power structure. The Grub Street authors were "combustible at any time" because of their antagonism with the status quo.[70] Marc-Antoine, too, tried and failed to become a well-known man of letters. His personality was far from combustible, and his political career evidences more tact and patience than his passionate writing about Rousseau might indicate. But to classify him as a future revolutionary in the 1770s and 1780s is surely just.[71]

Rosalie loved Marc-Antoine for his virtue and his values. She undoubtedly shared many of his opinions. However, in her private letters, she demonstrated less precision in her criticism of French society than Marc-Antoine did in his letters to philosopher friends. If she was less pragmatic, she was no less touched by the spirit of the Enlightenment. She was an enlightened women by virtue of her optimism, her "daring to know" through great quantities of reading, her interest in science evidenced by her silkworm experiments, her reverence for virtue, and her belief in humankind's potential. She was particularly aware of her children's potential. Although her gender prevented her from becoming a man of letters, her maternal devotion to her sons and her aspirations for their careers made her a likely future revolutionary as well. Her reading provided her an alternative vision of French society where talent and virtue were more important than wealth or birth. But this desire for change does not equate to an expectation of change.

3

The Beginning of the Revolution

IN THE GAP in letters between October 1787 and August 1789, much transpired in Rosalie's life. In the winter of 1785, Rosalie and Auguste joined Marc-Antoine and Jules in Paris, where they stayed at least through October 1787. By August 1789, however, Rosalie and Jules were staying with her friend Madame Dejean in Versailles, and Marc-Antoine and Auguste were back in Romans. They all might have left Paris earlier in the summer, before any revolutionary events occurred, Marc-Antoine heading south to family and Rosalie making a friendly visit en route. Maybe they left Paris after the storming of the Bastille because they were uncomfortable with the violence in the capital. Or maybe they were drawn to Versailles, where the new National Assembly was meeting and where news had the shortest distance to travel to their curious ears. In any case, by August 1789, Rosalie was still very confused and frightened about what was happening around her.

Political changes were also numerous in this nearly two-year gap. The Prerevolution was a period from January 1787 to May 1789 that was marked by constant erosion of the monarchy owing to financial fiascos, the actions of unruly nobles, and a proliferation of pamphlets emanating from courts, lawyers, and elite members of the Third Estate. By the time the delegates from the Third Estate took the Tennis Court Oath in June 1789, the unrest among political elites, fear and hunger among most of the rest of the population, and lack of leadership on the part of the king had combined explosively.

In the first two years of the Revolution, the revolutionaries elaborated their liberal program. Among their accomplishments were the Declaration of the Rights of Man and of the Citizen, the appropriation and sale of Church land to fund a new currency, and the Constitution. They also faced challenges when the popular classes exerted their strength: successfully in the October Days when crowds brought the king to Paris, disastrously in the Champ de Mars Massacre when protesters were attacked. The greatest challenge of all was the king's flight in June 1791, which seemed to sap the Constitution of its potency and decisively drove a wedge not only between royalists and revolutionaries but also between radicals who wanted to unseat Louis and moderates who preferred a constitutional monarchy to the threat of anarchy.[1]

Rosalie's letters from this two-year period, 1789–1791, are intermittent. Her first letter following the onset of revolution is dated August 27, 1789. Next there are four from September and one dated October 5, 1789. Another large gap separates that letter from the next, dated April 4, 1790. She wrote four letters in August 1791, five in September, and four in October. And then there is no correspondence until April 1792. In these two years, Rosalie's missives are like thinly scattered stars across a dark sky, some lonely, some haphazardly clumped. It is up to us to trace the lines that give meaning to the constellation of her first revolutionary experience. Although these stars offer only dim light, a revolutionary takes shape in the shadows.

"I have so many things to tell you, my good friend, and my heart is so full that my paper and plume seem like cold instruments with which to spill into your bosom all of the different feelings that animate me," Rosalie opened her first revolutionary letter, addressed to Marc-Antoine en route to Romans.[2] It was in fact a short letter—two large pages instead of a more typical four—and it was more jumbled than normal. Who could blame her for her disorganization? It mirrored the fast pace of the events that were under way in the brand new National Constituent Assembly.

She wrote on August 27, the day after the Declaration of the Rights of Man and of the Citizen was adopted. The Declaration has been described as a triumph for the bourgeoisie: it codified liberal values, including the inviolability of private property, and it ended the Old Regime social order by making everyone equal before the law.[3] It was the latter achievement that pleased Rosalie. This immense change in the legal system of France was sure to give her sons opportunities that she had not dared to hope for. But the significance of this achievement did not sink in immediately. She wrote Marc-Antoine briefly, "They finished the Rights of Man [and of the Citizen] today, and the first words of the great and immortal Constitution. Everyone is waiting for it impatiently."[4]

This good news was mixed with anxious feelings as she explained how disorganized she believed her surroundings were. "The shortage of bread that continues in Paris" was a "curse" of which she was "fearful." In an effort to understand the situation better, she visited a friend and "two deputies of the Clergy," but "I did not hear anything reassuring or satisfactory." She also tried to discuss events with other friends, but she was equally dissatisfied: "Yesterday at Madame Coqueret's house I heard twelve knowledgeable people think through everything that has happened. The opinions were so diverse that a poor spirit looking for the right one was in a quandary.... One is sick of talking because of the chatter. I didn't open my mouth yesterday."[5]

The majority of her letter discussed this frustration. In addition to the Declaration, the clamors for bread, and the cacophony of disagreement, Rosalie also quickly mentioned the abbé Sieyès, the compte de Mirabeau, and clergymen who protested attacks on their autonomy. All of these topics received the briefest of notes. She elaborated again on her confusion: "My friend, we are tossed by so many different winds, we are agitated by so many different passions, we are moved by such powerful interests, that the whirlwind crashes and breaks like the most violent storm. The lightening of truth, will it emerge from all of this? I hope so." Finally, she ended her quickly composed letter: "They are talking about paper money as a good resource. At last, my good friend, they talk about so many things that it is impossible to repeat everything. Write me very soon, I am waiting for your news with the greatest impatience.... Adieu, tender friend, adieu dear spouse, I do not have time to reread my letter."[6]

At the end of August, Rosalie was interested only in collecting information, staying away from "Paris, where I am afraid," and listening selectively to the diverse opinions she encountered.[7] Jules, meanwhile, was already exhilarated. As she wrote, he was at the Assembly. For the next two years, he would attend the meetings and report to his mother, who wrote to family and friends about the results. In the beginning, it seems fourteen-year-old Jules helped Rosalie to learn about and think through events the most. Perhaps her conversations with him, forever a disciple of Rousseau, led her to make this single political statement, in which she defined virtuous leadership: "passionate oratory and calm wisdom, the great principles of justice and the perfect abnegation of every other goal and interest outside of the public good."[8] She hoped such leadership would emerge.

Jules went "continuously to the National Assembly," but how nervous Rosalie remained.[9] The violence of the crowds unsettled her. The Great Fear in the provinces led peasants to revolt against the nobles. Rumors of brigands continued. On September 1, she wrote, "The day before yesterday, they stopped carriages filled with guns, powder, and bullets that were going, they say, to the brigands. They were turned away from Sève and taken to Paris. Who sent them? Where? The veil of the most somber politics covers it all. The National Guard is active in Paris and its environs, but thank heaven there has not been bloodshed yet. I have such respect for human blood that I do not want one drop spilled." She did not sleep at all that night because she worried about violence.[10]

Her nervousness prevented her from leaving the Dejeans' home in Versailles. She went with Jules once to the National Assembly and then quickly declared, "I will not go voluntarily to the Assembly because of… the terrible shock of passions that are in motion there. I only went once, and the profound impression that it left at the bottom of my soul will never fade."[11] She was so unhappy that she wanted to go home to Romans. She spent several letters asking Marc-Antoine for his permission to bring Jules back with her. She worried about the availability of food in the winter, about her safety, and about the separation she and her husband were about to endure.

> We have six months of winter to get through. Our cottages in
> Dauphiné offer us free refuge. Our retreat in Paris does not offer
> us the same thing, and we might not have bread. Think about it

again, my beloved. . . . Without a change in events, there might
be so many unfortunate people here, and that alone is making
many people leave. Twenty people told me that in our situation, they would not hesitate a moment. It is time already. Look
and judge. I do not fear the voyage despite my bad health, and
I await, whimpering, your last orders because you might have
something to recommend. . . . We would be better in Dauphiné
than here.[12]

She did not leave. Marc-Antoine did not respond quickly, her health
was rather poor, and it is possible that Jules fought for the chance to
stay. He continued to go often to the National Assembly. Rosalie was
in their home in Paris, in Saint-Germain, by September 10, when she
wrote to Marc-Antoine, "I wanted to ask you if you think it is good
that I let Jules go to Versailles to attend the Assembly and stay the night
with Madame Dejean." Then, echoing the report she had just given him
about the Assembly's debates over the king's veto power, she added, "I
would not let him take this adult step without your royal sanction, and
I give you an absolute veto, my good friend."[13]

Her joking was short-lived, as she continued to express anxiety
over living in Paris. At the end of the month, she told Marc-Antoine,
"I would rather live in a hole in the middle of a field than in a palace in the middle of the capital." But Jules was taken by the revolutionary spectacle. "Jules is dying for a uniform," Rosalie wrote. He
watched the ceremonial reviews of troops, "which are frequent," and
which "spurred his young courage." "The sword and the gun seem to
him to be the only way to happiness."[14] Rosalie's way to happiness was
blocked. She still wanted to return to Dauphiné, but Marc-Antoine
had finally written a response. He wanted to continue with their plan,
by which Rosalie would live in Paris with Jules so he could continue
attending his school, and Marc-Antoine and Auguste would stay in
Romans. Rosalie acquiesced. "We must follow Providence blindly,
and not leave the post that she marked for us until our tasks are com-
pleted. If we have misfortune, we will . . . suffer it with courage. What
will be, will be."[15]

What was, was the October Days. On October 5, thousands of women from the popular classes marched twelve miles from Paris to Versailles with a concise list of complaints and demands. They wanted better bread supply, they maligned the clergymen who were holding up reform, and ultimately they wanted the king to relocate to Paris, where he would be free of bad advisers and would ensure the well-being of the people. The march was a dramatic event; it has been memorialized in images and studied by historians because of its undeniably gendered nature.[16]

Rosalie wrote to Marc-Antoine on the evening of October 5: "This morning, Paris was as agitated as it was on the famous 14 and 15 of July. The food shortage, which has had us by the throat for four days, disheartens everyone. Then an anecdote arrived from Versailles. They say that the king's guards and the officers from the Regiment of Flanders trampled on the national banner." The rumor of this action and the news of the ample feast that the troops had enjoyed while the Parisians worried over bread had in fact spurred the women of Paris to action. Rosalie reported on the mixed crowd that first gathered in the city. "The Faubourg Saint Antoine, the Dames de la Halle, an innumerable cohort of citizens of every rank from the capital, of every sex, of every age poured down the streets here, there, and everywhere. Hunger from one corner, terror from another. There is nothing as pitiful as this spectacle and nothing as frightening as the scene that it produces."[17]

Crowds were familiar to Rosalie, who had lived in Paris at different points throughout her life. But mobs were a different matter. Historians debate the nature of the revolutionary crowds, some assigning them more rationality and order than others. Rosalie, too, would come to change her mind about the safety and respectability of popular protests. In 1789, however, "mob" was her term, and she found it "frightening."[18]

While most accounts described the marchers as almost exclusively female, Rosalie did not. "They all went to Versailles. At four o'clock, men, women, troops, canons, and Monsieur de La Fayette at their head in spite of himself, after exhausting all of his eloquence to suppress this enthusiasm and stop this march. God Almighty, watch over everyone!" As she wrote that evening, "the calm [was] profound." She waited and wondered what would transpire. "Friends of men and of humanity, brothers and citizens, where are you going?" The event caused her to change her mind about leaving her post in Paris. "What is keeping us here? Not home or commerce or money. Our children?" Auguste was already with Marc-Antoine, and she said that Jules's classes, which were supposed to start the next day, might be postponed because of the "fear of famine." Concern over food supply worried Rosalie considerably. She reminded Marc-Antoine that "together, hunger and cold might wage war on us" that winter. It would be easy for her to leave: "[O]ne small trunk and I am gone." This thought led to another bit of wisdom: "[P]overty of possessions, you alone give us liberty."[19]

Before going to sleep, Rosalie added a postscript: "At ten o'clock they said that a new troop of men and women left again for Versailles to ask the king to come live in the Louvre. They will not return without him. They are worried the king will leave from another direction. Heads are hot. We need more than a winter's snow to cool them. I am not at ease." The next morning, she wrote incredulously, "The news from Versailles is superb." The king and his family were on their way to Paris. She was not yet calm, however. "Our enemies are turned away, but they are not vanquished. Clouds and storms keep coming, misery and hunger will return.... In Dauphiné we have food and shelter for almost nothing, for no trouble, no famine. Here eight thousand souls go hungry when there is no bread."[20] Her feelings of fear were more pronounced than any sense of excitement for this step in the Revolution.

There her letters from 1789 stop, not to resume again, in the archive, until April 1790. Maybe Rosalie was finally successful at getting Marc-Antoine to change his mind, and she went home for the winter. Two letters from April 1790 provide a brief glimpse of her thoughts on the Revolution nearly a year after its beginning. The changes in her attitude are staggering. In the fall of 1789, both the threat of hunger and the uncertainty of crowd behavior brought Rosalie to beg again and again for a new plan, one that would allow the family to live together in Romans. Aside from this topic, Rosalie wrote little about politics. She had few opinions, few hopes. The next spring, she wrote again from Paris, where Marc-Antoine and the boys were also now living. If she had in fact spent the previous winter outside the capital, that did not prevent her from becoming knowledgeable, and opinionated, about current events.

Rosalie had new thoughts on the crowds. She wrote to Virginie, "The people of Paris know that they must respect the sacred character of the [Constituent Assembly] deputies." She was so reassured of the popular classes' restraint that she compared them to Montesquieu's allegorical Troglodytes, a tribe whose members governed themselves virtuously for the good of the community.[21] The peasants also grew in her esteem. Rosalie told Virginie a "real story." "A wealthy peasant near La Rochelle was elected the mayor of his village. His uprightness and his virtues brought him there. After fifteen days, he said he could no longer fill that position because his children, who were still small, could not plow his field. The commune assembled, learned the situation of this honest citizen, and, moved by his virtues, they reached this generous resolution: everyone of us, they said, gives you one day out of the week, and we would consider it a pleasure to work free of charge for our brave mayor! The whole assembly applauded, and the virtuous citizen went gloriously home to his cottage."[22] She wrote that this story brought her to tears.

She was so optimistic, she was giddy. In place of fear was a sense of humor. Virginie had written to Marc-Antoine, but it was Rosalie who responded because "French gallantry was, thank goodness, abolished by the new rights of man," and so Marc-Antoine felt "no scruples" in leaving her without a response. "At your service, my dear friend, I speak in his place," she continued.[23]

But Rosalie was humorless about aristocrats. In March 1790, the Constituent Assembly published and disseminated the king's financial report. Known as the *livre rouge*, the report contained the king's record of expenditure, including pensions for his family members, servants of the court, and a considerable number of aristocrats throughout the country. The extravagance of the aristocrats' lifestyle contrasted with the humility of the virtuous peasants Rosalie had just described. This dynamic raised her esteem for the poor and invigorated her contempt for the aristocracy. She told Virginie, "We have the *livre rouge*, which reveals the cupidity and baseness of our leaders. Our poor country people sweat blood and tears to furnish these vampires of the court with their corrupt luxury."[24] Her disgust at the court's excesses quickly spread to hate for all aristocrats. She told Virginie that the Constitution could be "one of the most splendid spectacles that history ever presented. But the aristocrats...put up so many obstacles, employ so many ruses, create so many horrors, that friends of humanity and truth and justice cannot look at them without being seized by indignation and wrath." She concluded, "All of Milton's devils are angels in comparison to the devilish aristocracy."[25]

Her views had grown so fierce, in fact, that a dear friend complained about the Julliens' obsession with the aristocracy. In July 1790, during a summer from which there is only one, not particularly interesting, letter from Rosalie, we gain the most insight from Saint-Cyr Nugues, who visited the Julliens' home while still at boarding school in Paris. After one visit, he wrote the following complaint to his father:

Several days ago I went to Monsieur Jullien's house....I ask you only to observe that my actions have always been patriotic like everyone else's. I gave my silver buckles to the contribution. I prayed with all my comrades during the civic sermon. My *aristocratic nature*, to the extent that it is aristocratic, is therefore part of my interior sentiment: and perhaps the democrats did not donate their buckles....No one knows the obligations that I owe to [Monsieur Jullien] better than I, all the gratitude and friendship I owe to his family. However, I cannot stop myself from finding some of his claims incorrect: that he said, for example, that at [school] I am in *a quagmire*...that Madame Jullien tells me that she pardons the aristocrats who die from the Revolution, but that she *detests* those, like me, who embrace this party; that Jules comes to see me and talk with me in order to report our conversation to his father because what I said was reprehensible; that Auguste comes to me and accuses our school of having us write

"*Vive le roi*" above the door in four languages; and a thousand other similar annoyances that are no more true than the others.... [Madame Jullien] told me that I am pitiable, that she pities me; Jules comes with a haughty air to assure me that they know my patriotism and that no one doubts it, or he gives me some pamphlets that defame Monsieur Dubertrand [his teacher] and the school; Auguste scowls at me or traps me in the corner to call me "*aristocratic villain.*" I cannot do anything but keep silent.[26]

Saint-Cyr claimed that the Julliens concocted accusations against him, Jules spied on him, and little Auguste sneered from the corners of the house. He contended to his father that his donation of his silver buckles was a greater sign of patriotism than he saw from "the democrats," the Julliens. But the Julliens worried that he sympathized with the aristocrats because of rumors of his lessons in school. To the young Saint-Cyr, the Julliens appeared severe, accusatory, self-righteous, and willing to suspect even their closest friends of counterrevolutionary offenses.

It is tempting to see this conflict as an outgrowth of the concern Rosalie had expressed in the 1780s about the effect of the Nugueses' wealth on their virtue. Perhaps during the Revolution, the discomfort Rosalie had always had with luxury was amplified to the point of alienating old friends. It is not unreasonable to assume that the Julliens felt some jealousy or embarrassment about the modesty of their fortune compared to that of the Nugueses. Later, Rosalie comforted herself and Jules by writing defensively, "We are not reduced to putting gold in the place of feeling like these foolish and stupid rich."[27] Because revolutionary culture valued feelings and intentions, one could be an excellent revolutionary without being a generous donor. The Julliens' wealth did not restrict their patriotism.

However, the Nugueses remained dear friends of the Julliens, and Jules and Saint-Cyr wrote each other affectionately during their trials as young adults and aspiring politicians. Rather than demonstrating a drastic change in the Julliens' personal relationships, this episode shows that political disagreements could become very personal. The Julliens believed Saint-Cyr's teacher was promoting aristocratic values. Saint-Cyr defended his teacher and his school. The difference between good and evil, patriots and aristocrats, seemed so black-and-white to the Julliens that their friends' affinity for a rumored aristocrat caused considerable tension, for a moment.

Jules, on the other hand, concocted a plan to leave school altogether. While in Romans in the late summer of 1791, he wrote to his parents to declare that he was staying. He would become a much better citizen, he argued, if he designed his own education outside Paris and away from the corruption of civil society. In a natural environment, he could commit himself to "different work projects that I would follow consistently." After three months of recovering from the "duties of society that robbed me of a thousand precious moments," he would enter, "according to my taste," into reading his books. Then he would spend a year in the service of a government official, and then a year in England, presumably to study the British constitutional government. Rosalie was vexed, called him "ungrateful," and vetoed his plans.[28] His moment of rebellion subsided.

The Julliens' fear of aristocratic conspiracies places them on the left of the political spectrum.[29] It is curious that a devoted Catholic such as Rosalie felt comfortable in that position. A major feature of this first phase of the Revolution was an attack on the Church. The Civil Constitution of the Clergy, issued on July 12, 1790, dramatically reduced the autonomy of the Church. The government limited the number of bishops and mandated lay elections of Church officials. It also began to pay priests' salaries, making them servants of the state, which was necessary after the revolutionaries banned the tithe in early August 1789. On November 27, 1790, the government required the secular clergy to swear an oath to the Civil Constitution. In doing so, they proclaimed their allegiance to France above all else.

Many Frenchmen and -women protested these laws. Counterrevolutionary nuns were particularly vocal in their opposition. In part, this was because they were especially targeted. A decree of March 20, 1790, required nuns to agree to be interrogated as to their intentions to join and stay in the convent, reflecting the influence of Denis Diderot's novel about a nun who was forced into a convent where girls were being tyrannized by the mother superior.[30] For the revolutionaries, convents symbolized "religious zeal and royalist fervor," elements that threatened the Revolution's progress.[31] The association between women and religion, and between women and irrationality, was strong in political rhetoric, and it reflected the mistrust of the nuns on the part of the political leaders.[32]

Eventually, the attack on religion would also fuel violent counter-revolution in the Vendée. But clergymen elsewhere did not protest the Civil Constitution. In fact, in a diocese in Marc-Antoine's home province of Dauphiné, 88 percent of the clergy swore the oath, and southeastern France in general had proportionally some of the highest numbers of juring, or swearing, priests.[33] Those parish priests saw the Revolution as beneficial to their well-being, which had lingered on the edge of desperation in recent decades because of unreliable income and uneven distribution of the Church's money.[34] Those curés had sent a proposal for Church reform to the National Assembly on September 2, 1789.[35] When the government wrote the Civil Constitution of the Clergy, the curés' position in the community was boosted because, as Tackett observes, they were being paid not by "pompous non-resident tithe owners but by the 'French Nation.'"[36] As for the theological dilemma of pledging allegiance to a secular authority, Tackett notes, the clergy in Dauphiné had already "grown accustomed to bypassing the bishops and the ecclesiastical hierarchy and to appealing directly to…civil authorities.…In the age-old struggle between Church and State, the Dauphine curés had, in a sense, already opted for the state."[37] They saw themselves "not only as men of God, but as public servants as 'the first and most perfect citizens.'"[38]

As a former resident of Dauphiné and a dedicated Enlightenment reader, Rosalie seems also to have adopted this utilitarian stance on the Church. She grew increasingly frustrated with the clergy who balked at the state's intervention and, through their protests, threatened to cause discord throughout the country. In April 1790, Rosalie wrote to Virginie about the government's plan to sell Church property to finance the new currency, the assignat. She wrote this letter after the measure had been fiercely debated, further galvanized by a monk who, on April 12, moved to make Catholicism the state religion. The debate was "as tumultuous as any to date," according to a historian of the Constituent Assembly, and was finally resolved by a victory by the Left, defeating the motion.[39] Rosalie blamed the priests for acting greedily and atrociously, calling them unworthy servants of a peace-loving god. Worrying that they would attract the common people to their cause and bring about more bloodshed, she wrote: "The clergy moved heaven and earth these last fifteen days of Easter, not to save but to damn, along with themselves, all of those who are stupid enough in the National Assembly to believe them.... They raged for three days. They made scandalous scenes in public. They tried to mask their own interests as the interests of Religion."[40] Rosalie never expressed anticlerical attitudes in the Old Regime, but as the clergy divided during the Revolution, she readily attacked the counterrevolutionaries.

In spite of those feelings, her faith remained strong. Religion continued to comfort her in times of hardship. When Auguste was very sick with a high fever in August 1791, she ceased discussing politics in three successive letters and wrote only about him, her efforts to alleviate his fever, and her gratitude for God's help. "Saintly religion, you alone are the support for the unhappy," she professed. Next, in response to news that a young friend had died, she comforted Jules contemplatively: "*Voilà* the life of man, my son... it is full of thorns.... I know a fortress that is impenetrable to the strokes of fortune. It is religion, my son. That is the sacred sanctuary where the despairing find solid consolation."[41] In this period of anticlericalism that had not yet become outright de-Christianization, Rosalie was content both with the Church reforms and with her uninterrupted faithful practices.

On June 20, 1791, an event that would forever change the course of the Revolution took place. The king and his family fled Paris, intent on reaching allies across the eastern border, to stop the Revolution. At first, there was confusion. Had the king been abducted? Then, nearly at the edge of his empire, Louis was spotted in Varennes, and he was returned to Paris as a prisoner. The popular attitude toward the king, the "good king poorly advised," changed instantly and forever at that moment. He had already faced threats in Paris. One reason for his flight was a series of popular uprisings: on the royal prison in Vincennes in February 1791, on his retinue in April when he tried to attend Easter services with nonjuring clergy in Saint-Cloud, and infinite numbers of smaller skirmishes throughout the spring. The sections of Paris were meeting constantly. The Cordelier Club, led by such incendiaries as Marat, Desmoulins, and Danton, was recruiting people from the popular classes on the Left Bank. The crowds' strength was undeniable, and it intimidated moderates as well as royalists. They wanted discipline; the radicals wanted expanded democracy. The king wanted to escape.[42]

After his flight, some groups within and outside the capital immediately called for a republic. Violence raged here and there in the provinces as priests and nobles were attacked. Louis was returned to Paris on June 25, and that day the Constituent Assembly began to debate what should be done with him. The Left declared that to allow royal immunity would be to leave the door open for another Nero. Jérôme Pétion and Maximilien Robespierre especially championed the progressives' cause, opposing royal immunity and most moderate measures to contain the power of the people of Paris. But the Constitution was nearly complete, and it held a place for a constitutional monarch.

On July 16, the Assembly decided to reinstate the king once the Constitution was complete, which it was on September 3. The Cordelier Club immediately petitioned the Assembly to reconsider. As crowds protested and assembled in the Champ de Mars, the mayor of Paris ordered martial law. The Champ de Mars Massacre that resulted on July 17, in which probably fifty demonstrators were killed, severely dampened the morale of patriots such as Rosalie. Following the Massacre, she told Marc-Antoine, "As I would like to die of natural causes and not be a martyr to my feelings," she was keeping her opinions to herself.[43]

Rosalie's correspondence resumes in August 1791, after a hiatus of nearly a year. She rarely mentioned the king in her letters before his flight. In one moment of enthusiasm, she reported that the "Good King" had asked for the tricolor banner to be flown throughout the empire and that France was following the history of England on its way to constitutional monarchy.[44] After the king's flight, she wrote in August 1791 that she believed he would continue to try to flee. To

Jules she wrote, "I would not be surprised to have to tell you soon that Monsieur Louis XVI is leaving, has left, etc. etc., and that the guard that is stationed at the door of the Louvre did not know anything."[45] As the Constitution neared completion, waiting for Louis's approval, Rosalie quoted La Fontaine: "C'était assez de biens; mais quoi / Rien ne remplit les vastes appétits d'un Roi [There were enough goods, but so what / Nothing satisfies a king's large appetite]."[46] She doubted he would be the constitutional monarch they had hoped for.

Although Rosalie discussed the king infrequently in her letters, she and Marc-Antoine had certainly been among those calling for his removal. Marc-Antoine had joined the Jacobin Club by now, and some of his colleagues there were among Rosalie's most admired revolutionaries: Robespierre, Pétion, and Buzot.[47] In August, Jules spent some time with their family in Romans and joined the Jacobin Club there. Rosalie wrote eagerly asking for his report on their meetings.[48] Certainly Marc-Antoine's affection for Rousseau and Mably played a part in his vision for the New Regime, which was almost definitely not a monarchy. Rosalie sounded as if she regretted the decision to maintain the monarchy in the 1791 Constitution when she wrote, "We must descend again to the common level and realize that the best is the enemy of the good," meaning a good compromise was better than nothing. Therefore, "I join the animals of all types under the sacred arc of the Constitution."[49]

For her part, Rosalie gathered news and formed opinions by reading newspapers and talking with neighbors and friends. She read widely, including Marat's paper, *L'Ami du Peuple*, whose rants she did not like. She preferred the more moderate *Journal de Paris* and the *Moniteur*.[50] Her neighbors sometimes passed news to her through her window, and her good friends Tiberge and Dejean visited often to discuss personal and political matters.[51]

Rosalie's growing sense of understanding the Revolution resulted in a significant change of attitude by the summer of 1791. Her initial feelings of fear and confusion were replaced by excitement and optimism. While she had no political ideology in 1789, by 1791, she was not only pro-revolutionary, but she also favored the politics of the Left. This position included a revision of her attitude toward the urban crowds. Jacobin ideology favored greater democracy, universal male suffrage, and support of the people of Paris when they fought for their demands. Perhaps because of the influence of Marc-Antoine and Jules—the two card-carrying Jacobins in the family—she warmed up to the crowds. She also felt fortunate to be living in Paris. After a short holiday in Pontoise, she wrote, "I have to tell you that the people in the provinces see the Revolution like those who are seated at the opera staring at the stage. We Parisians can see what happens in the wings. We see the actors change their costume, their role, and we see the cords that lift the gods to Olympus."[52]

Rosalie enjoyed reporting on life in Paris while Jules and Marc-Antoine were in Romans. She probably suspected that her letters to them would be read in the local Jacobin Club, adding to her sense of participation in political discourse. This new purpose for her correspondence is likely the reason behind an elevation in her prose. She easily commanded the rhetoric around her and wrote eloquently to Jules, "Everywhere I go, public spirit is full of wise and sweet moderation. They adore the Constitution, they admire the National Assembly, they see the end in sight.... Our constancy and our courage will vanquish everything. Love for the Constitution brings all hearts to a space of heroism. For that, public spirit is mature and ready."[53] Further addressing her Jacobin son and his colleagues, she wrote another time about support for the Constitution on the part of the "masses [who] are pure like the air of our fields."[54] Rosalie was no longer a spectator. She was a spokesperson.[55]

This metamorphosis is striking because while she evolved, she also described the transformation around her. In fact, a charming motif runs throughout these letters. A student of sericulture, Rosalie was familiar with metamorphosis. She drew on that experience when she discussed history in terms of inevitable progress. This stance lent her patience and optimism, because even as some ideals, like republicanism, were "too elevated for others," there was hope in the fact that "the most common [people] have traveled a century in the last ten years."[56] It was not only the popular classes that were evolving. The assemblymen, too, were "still a little like the Huron when [trying to be] a Roman or Spartan in Paris."[57] But when Rosalie considered "the general corruption and the degradation of men withered by twelve centuries of slavery," she hoped that "in time regeneration will succeed despite all of the obstacles."[58] Thinking back to her experience with the silk worms, she trusted, "That will come. It takes more than a day to transform certain butterflies."[59]

Her increasingly well-composed letters incorporated images that she recalled from her life in Romans. When discussing her excitement for the Constitution, she borrowed this metaphor from La Fontaine: "The oak breaks, but the reed bends. The reed is our constitution. It bends, but it is not destroyed. I have seen it resist all manner of wind, and it holds, a little tattered, against the fury of every storm."[60] Despite her disagreement with the decision to allow Louis to keep his executive position, Rosalie was inspired by the Constitution and certain that it set the foundation for future evolutions in French society.

By the end of 1791, Rosalie's understanding of and stance toward the Revolution had evolved from anxiety to enthusiasm. Her initial hesitancy can probably be attributed to the fact that she never expected such change would happen in her lifetime. The same was not true of all future revolutionaries. Five men who were also middle-class and well educated left bodies of correspondence from the prerevolutionary period.[61] Unlike Rosalie, by the time the Assembly of Notables was called in February 1787, they realized that the potential for revolutionary changes was real. As the Estates General met, they became, as Tackett describes them, more "political, partisan, and radical."[62] They began to express opinions as if their voices mattered. Rosalie and Marc-Antoine knew personally the philosopher who had written a hopeful script for a revolution that was starting to take shape in 1787, and yet Rosalie was not prepared for the changes of 1789, nor did she hold any expectations after it began.

Despite this initial reticence, Rosalie eventually developed a political identity as a Jacobin. Her husband's and son's enthusiasm surely played a part in her migration to the Left. Although she rarely referenced Enlightenment thinkers in her letters, Marc-Antoine was deeply involved in Enlightenment discourse. In their spoken conversations, Rosalie and Marc-Antoine probably began to think of the Revolution in terms of that reading. Equally as important were her experiences. If her growing confidence in the natural goodness of the common people derived from Rousseau, her personal experiences reinforced those beliefs. She seems to have collected most of her data secondhand, from friends, neighbors, and newspapers, but those reports accompanied her observations from her window and led her to believe in the people's preparedness for a New Regime.

Finally, by August 1791, she went fearlessly to a public place. After partaking in a "superb festival on the Champs Elysée," she exclaimed that "the capital has never been more brilliant, dazzling, magnificent, dancing, adorned, [or] opulent."[63] And although the following month she still called Romans "our universe," she also tended to report more often about the feeling of the city, as if she were part of the public spirit.[64] She wrote once, for example, "Paris is calm like the surface of a pond, aside from certain ripples that cause, every day, scenes of tragedy."[65] It was with a poetic eye that Rosalie surveyed the landscape, determined now to take her place as a revolutionary.

4

Radicalization

IN EIGHTEENTH-CENTURY FRANCE, the Petite Poste circulated mail within Paris. The Grande Poste system sent mail beyond the capital, to the provinces and abroad. Its headquarters in Paris, the stately Hôtel des Postes, sat on the rue Platrière. It boasted a large courtyard lined with columns and grand staircases dotted with bronze fleurs-de-lis. Seventy-eight Grande Poste mailboxes were scattered throughout Paris, many in shops and bakeries. Two hundred mailmen emptied these boxes every morning at eight o'clock. The Revolution did not disrupt this system; in fact, it streamlined and expanded it. Letters for which the postage was to be paid by the recipient could be left in the boxes. When a letter, such as one destined for London, required postage, the sender had to enter the ornate Hôtel des Postes to pay its way. The post left from Paris for London every Monday and Thursday.[1] Twice a week in 1792, one of the two hundred postal workers received a letter destined to cross the English Channel from a conscientious *épistolière*.[2]

Jules made it to London after all. He left Paris in May. He was there ostensibly to study, but in truth, adults in his life had planned his journey for other reasons. Rosalie hoped this move would prevent him from joining the army and help his career in politics and journalism. She remembered the gleam in her boy's eyes as he watched the uniformed soldiers march through Paris in 1789. She explained to Marc-Antoine, "My son's voyage to England was for me simply a measure of prudence to distance him from the military.... I saw [General] La Fayette as the executioner of France's youth."[3] In April, France started a long and increasingly global war. Jules had returned to Paris from Romans at some point in the winter or spring of 1792. His patriotic fervor had only grown since 1789, and it made Rosalie nervous. On the other hand, leaders in France hoped that Jules could gather intelligence abroad.[4]

Jules joined the Jacobin Club in the capital, as he had done in Romans. His membership card from 1792 depicts a youth whose enthusiasm had only grown during three years of Revolution. On this card, he wrote that his profession was "youth, writer, patriot." Under "patriotic service and titles," he declared, not exactly accurately, "I was one of the first to take up arms in the first days of our liberty. Since that time, as a member of several Societies of the Friends of the Constitution [now called Jacobins], I have always exhibited the true principles of true patriots." After he signed the bottom line, he added in the margin: "Real patriots, firm friends of the Revolution, are those who wanted it before it came, who anticipated it with their desires, and for whom the *patrie* was not just a fanciful idea even though the word *patrie* was hardly a French word at all. Yes, I can pride myself on being one of those pure and true patriots, invariable in their principles, because I was a friend of the constitution before there was a constitution." He signed again, "Jullien," and, still not done, added a final thought: "I swear to be faithful to the nation and the law and to defend, with my life, the Declaration of the Rights of Man. I promise to observe the rules of the Society. I declare that I will never join the Feuillants."[5] His exuberance and his desire to be a "writer" were evident even on this small card.

Marc-Antoine, on the other hand, was almost entirely consumed with family affairs, and he did not have Rosalie's support. His younger sister was experiencing trouble with her mills and other financial concerns. Although Rosalie did not think that Marc-Antoine needed to help her (several of Marc-Antoine's siblings lived nearby already), Marc-Antoine spent a great deal of time back home. He had attempted to win election to the Legislative Assembly in the fall of 1791. At that time, Rosalie had said it was perhaps a gift from God that he lost.[6] She did not realize that his defeat meant his return to Romans.

For the first time, Rosalie was nearly alone in Paris, to partake in the Revolution on her own terms. Jules would no longer go daily to the National Assembly and report events to her. She began going herself, with young Auguste and their domestic servant, Marion. She spent

most days outside her home in search of activity in public places. "My
timid neighbors look at me with amazement that I dare cross my apartment's threshold," she told Jules proudly.[7] When Rosalie dared to cross
it, she witnessed some of the most significant events that transpired
during the Revolution. She wrote letters every few days detailing those
events for Jules. Jules made sure to save every one.

Rosalie spent the spring of 1792 collecting letters of introduction
and travel documents (so that Jules would not be mistaken for an émigré) to sweep him off to London. She hoped, she told her husband, "that
he learns to think in England before speaking and writing in France."[8]
Rosalie and Marc-Antoine did a splendid job of supplying Jules with
letters: Pétion, Dumouriez, Brissot, Condorcet, and Sillery wrote letters. Twenty deputies from the Legislative Assembly recommended him
for the task.[9] Jules stayed with a friend of a friend, Monsieur Demeuse,
who lived at no. 17 Crown Street in Soho. He learned English, made
some diplomatic contacts, and wrote to members of the political elite
about his observations.

Jules also met frequently with Lord Stanhope, an English earl known
for his sympathy for the French Revolution. It was this real-life figure
on whom Mably had modeled his character Lord Stanhope in his *Rights
and Duties of the Citizen*. The Lord Stanhope in that dialogue was an
English Commonwealth man who drew attention to France's inequali-
ties. What a thrill for the parents to see their son practically jump into
a scene from Mably's imagination. Rosalie wrote to Jules excitedly,
"I am penetrated with admiration for Milord Stanhope.... The welcome that he gave you reminded me of that which Mably gave your
father when he arrived in Paris under the same circumstances that you
arrived in London, searching instruction and science."[10] The next year,
Saint-Cyr Nugues mentioned Lord Stanhope in a letter to Jules, writing, "You must have been happy to ... see his morality and his character
in person."[11] Jules was happy about that, but homesickness and culture
shock were the main hallmarks of his seven months in London.

In Paris, the spring and summer of 1792 were marked by a deep
divide in the Legislative Assembly. While the Right supported the
court and the constitutional monarchy, the Left grew more prepared

to unseat the king. A powerful faction was committed to the constitu-
tional monarchy, but the numbers of militants in Paris were growing.
Tension accumulated in the spring, when food riots plagued Paris and
France declared war on Austria on April 20.

According to one theory, the dialectic of real and imagined enemies of the Revolution propelled the revolutionaries to greater and
greater extremes.[12] The foreign belligerents were unmistakably enemies of the revolutionary government. The revolutionaries, especially
those on the Left, also believed there were other enemies, conspirators
within France. Rosalie was privy to the conspiracy rumors that ebbed
in the winter of 1790–1791 and increased again as 1792 drew near.[13]
She was present when Jacques-Pierre Brissot and Armand Gensonné
announced on May 23, 1792, that an "Austrian Committee" was orches-
trating a grand conspiracy to extinguish the Revolution. She called
their speeches "superb" and those who needed more proof of such a
conspiracy "imbeciles." After all, "all harmful plotters...have enough
sense to plan their crimes in shadow and not leave any trace that could
lead to their conviction."[14] Rumor was enough to convince Rosalie of
the great conspiracy threat.[15]

Concern about enemies of the Revolution was the backdrop to three
events that occurred in 1792 and changed the nature of the Revolution
and the course of its history. The actors were the people of Paris, the
peuple, the sansculottes. This army, in Rosalie's estimation, defended
the Republic against bungling assemblymen, the machinations of the
court, and conspirators everywhere. The first event occurred in June,
and it marked a significant step in Rosalie's journey toward celebrating
the *peuple* as the key to the Revolution's success.[16]

The approach of two significant anniversaries stirred feelings in the
capital: those of the Tennis Court Oath of June 20, 1789, and the king's
flight at the end of June 1791. Cognizant of these anniversaries, Rosalie had
been expecting action for months. In May she reported, "[T]he storm is
growing here: all one talks about is plots, assassins, a Saint Bartholomew's
[Day Massacre] of patriots."[17] In early June, two critical acts by the king
galvanized the public: his dismissal of the "patriot" ministers around him
and their replacement with conservatives, and his refusal to allow armed

volunteers to assemble outside Paris to bolster defenses. Suspicion grew that the king was trying to undermine the Revolution. The storm hit on June 20, when thousands invaded the Tuileries Palace and demanded that the king assert his commitment to the Revolution.

The *journée* had begun as a peaceful procession of perhaps twenty-five thousand Parisians, originating in the eastern sections of the city and gathering strength en route to the Place Vendôme near the Legislative Assembly. Speakers complained about the king's vetoes and his dismissal of "patriot" ministers. They asserted their right to resist the tyranny of the executive power. The Assembly permitted the demonstrators to parade through the hall, carrying weapons, accompanied by a small orchestra playing patriotic songs. It seems that the assemblymen believed the crowd would return home after its message was communicated to the legislators. However, the march continued to the Tuileries Palace, where the royal family was cajoled into appearing. While not physically threatened, the king was compelled to toast the nation, and the great crowd of armed city dwellers left with satisfaction that evening.

The day before the *journée*, Rosalie described the scene she witnessed at the Legislative Assembly. On June 19, she felt the buildup: "Today the people wanted to go armed, as in '89, from the National Assembly to the Tuileries Palace, to present petitions. The Court, with its aristocratic prudence, promptly stopped all armed assembly…and made the mayor responsible for public security. Poor [Mayor] Pétion! Poor Pétion! What agony for your friends who see you between Charybdis and Scylla." She also added Marion's point of view: "Marion walked around the Tuileries yesterday evening. There were more people than grains of sand. Everyone spoke the same language. They strongly and rightly want the king either to support the Constitution or declare himself an enemy of it."[18]

The following day, June 20, she added to the same letter to Marc-Antoine and reported:

> What a wonderful day! What triumph! What protection from Heaven for a good people! I left [the Assembly] after eleven

o'clock and walked around the Place du Carrousel. I saw, with fright, three rows of cavalry flanking the walks and doors of the Château. An immense group of curious people filled the area from there to the National Assembly.... Poor Marion, outside, stayed at the Tuileries until seven o'clock. Thus you will know what happened everywhere because Marion has the eyes and ears of an observant philosopher. The National Assembly was never so brilliant or majestic; there was not an empty seat.... The *peuple* were there below; the real sovereign [the *peuple*] knew how to demonstrate a real majesty. Two hours passed in perfect tranquility. Citizens armed with pikes, national guardsmen, grenadiers, foot soldiers, ladies, women of the people, all mixed in a veritable spirit of equality and fraternal union.... Marion saw shocking things. The people were at the king's home. They presented him two cockades, one a tricolor and the other white [the Bourbon color]. Louis took the tricolor and donned a red cap.[19]

But Rosalie was quickly disappointed by the lack of results from this show of force. Not only did the king remain unchanged, but also Pétion was suspended from his position as punishment for the demonstration.

Consequently, Rosalie's praise for Pétion ("the incorruptible")[20] and the people ("the true sovereign") mounted. She argued that Pétion's alleged crime was *not* killing the thousands who marched on June 20. She wrote, "For some fools, kings' great crimes are petty, but the petty offenses of the people are great."[21] She viewed Pétion as on her side of the battle over the Constitution, aligned with the people against the court. In turn, the people (and "only" the people)[22] supported Pétion. She recalled a poorly organized and peaceful march after June 20 of one hundred thousand down the rue St-Honoré, above which she sat on a balcony. "What gave me the greatest pleasure was to see written, in white chalk on almost every hat, 'Vive Pétion.' This cry and that of 'Vive la Nation' were enthusiastically repeated."[23] Events such as this led her to conclude that the opinion of the common people was wiser than any philosopher.[24]

Not only were the *peuple* intelligent, but they were also civilized. She often related anecdotes such as this one from July: "A man of the people pushed me accidentally and offered me the most honorable excuses and walked a hundred feet with me to ask pardon. At the end of the street, he assured me that [the *peuple*] loved goodness and virtue so much that five thousand of them signed a request to reinstate brave Pétion. That is the *peuple*, my friend, and we can judge them by this [Roman] proverb: 'The voice of the *peuple* is the voice of God.'"[25] Evidence that the spirit of the Revolution had found refuge among the *peuple* was mounting. She professed that "vice lives in palaces," but "virtue hides under thatched [cottage] roofs."[26]

While Rosalie's affection for Pétion and the people grew, her loathing for the king also increased. On June 24, she wrote about the law preventing the people from arming themselves. She thought it was the work of the king, whose previous donning of the *bonnet rouge* was a lie and a "crime." His dismissal of Pétion was a declaration of war against the people and a move toward devastating the Constitution. She put it in violent terms: "Our [political] affairs are in the worst state I have ever seen because of the folly of certain people who claim that the Constitution was ravaged by the *peuple*, as if the king left it a virgin!"[27] For the first time, she wrote about his flight the previous year. She was furious about the way he had "deserted his post," which consequently "plunged the empire into the furors of civil war."[28] "It looks like he will again be King of France and not King of the French," she concluded, adding that not only was he not "of the French," but he also acted "against the people."[29] More commonly she referred to him as "Nero," or "Louis XIV."[30] When Pétion called for the king's deposition, she was delighted, writing that this would end discord in France.[31]

Her attitude toward the king inevitably made Rosalie more partisan. Just as the events of June 20 increased the ideological divides within the Legislative Assembly, Rosalie's stance drifted further left along with the radical Montagnards. She recounted a conversation with a Feuillant, who supported the decree that forbade the people to arm themselves and claimed that the militants of the popular classes were "brigands, or

what we used to call 'the dregs of the people.'" Rosalie responded that
to exclude the *peuple* from "the real [sovereign] people" was an act that
was "more dangerous than anything."[32] She also criticized the Feuillants
for adhering so strongly to the letter of the Constitution that they killed
its spirit. By insisting that the king had to be a part of the New Regime,
they made true liberty impossible. Out of this interpretation, Rosalie's
pride as a Jacobin grew. "These Jacobins are nothing if not the strongest columns of liberty and scarecrows for tyrants," she told Jules.[33] She
spent the day on August 5 at a meeting of the Jacobin Club and was so
impressed by the feeling of being at a Roman forum that she had trouble
leaving at nine thirty that night.[34]

Rosalie's reaction was indicative of the elevated and increasingly
polarized feelings toward the king after June 20. In fact, Rosalie's support of the people was a minority opinion in the context of France
as a whole, and even among some Parisians, who found the *journée*
dangerous and unnecessarily antagonistic. The Right, including the
Feuillants, gained adherents as they condemned the crowd and called
them "hordes of brigands." Meanwhile, Rosalie agreed with the less
popular Montagnards that the action was both peaceful and legitimate. Another split within the Left began to alienate Rosalie and her
family from some former friends who had written letters for Jules. The
Girondins vacillated on their stance toward the king, sometimes cling-
ing to the idea that he was a good king poorly advised, which angered
their former colleagues in the Mountain.

The divisions within the Legislative Assembly were growing
increasingly irreconcilable. Ultimately June 20 had little effect on the
king but a significant effect on the Assembly, whose members realized
that they were losing their grip on the course of events. At the end of
June, Lafayette appeared in the Legislative Assembly and declared that
the Jacobins must cede power and restore the sovereignty of the king.
The Right was buoyed and the Left enraged. Few knew that Lafayette,
previously a revolutionary hero and leader of the National Guard, had
been conspiring with the extreme Right in the Legislative Assembly to
march on Paris and extract the king.

Rosalie went to the Legislative Assembly often that summer. Its inability to make progress toward harmony frustrated her.[35] After June 20, petitions seeking the king's removal poured into the Assembly, but no vote took place while the moderate assemblymen floundered in indecision. Rosalie called the Legislative Assembly a "farce."[36] In July, the Assembly declared the *"patrie en danger,"* admitting that the war with Austria was putting France in peril. Troops from around the country were therefore encouraged to come to Paris for the July 14 celebration, which resulted in a mass assembly of a great diversity of patriots representing many corners of the country. This assembly of soldiers emboldened the people of Paris, who had been meeting constantly in their sections all summer. Inclined to take a holiday from the tension, Rosalie considered retreating to Pontoise just before the second and most significant event of the summer.[37]

In Paris, the Julliens lived in Saint-Germain, at the corner of rue Jacob and rue de Grenelle. From her window in this Left Bank apartment, Rosalie heard the tocsin sound when crowds gathered to take action against the monarchy. *Photo by author.*

On August 8, she made up her mind not to leave Paris after all. She explained to Jules, "I could stay at home perfectly well! I could easily walk through the countryside alone! But I have a certain curiosity in my heart that commands my steps to the places where there is often danger. The secret of sages is to know yourself well. Voilà. It is easier to follow than to resist."[38] The previous week had been filled with demonstrations and the drafting of petitions that demanded the removal of the king, a new constitution, and the indictment of Lafayette, among other things. On August 8, the Assembly gave Lafayette a vote of confidence, enraging the Parisian militants. The Tuileries buttressed its defenses.

The following night, the Paris sections planned their mobilization. Rosalie wrote a long letter to Virginie about what she saw and felt in the middle of the action to which she was drawn:

> The tocsin sounds, the call to arms is sung, the alarm rings. Throughout Paris the streets are full of people and the women tremble in their windows and timidly interrogate the passersby. What will happen? The vast population of the capital represents to the frightened imagination eight hundred thousand souls responding to all the horrors that the darkness of night increases. All the signals of terror are frightening. Death cannot be more poignant than the feeling of profound sadness that fills my soul.

The next morning she continued her letter, relieved that "the rays of daylight dissipated the fears of the night." Although she was unaware of events beginning to take place, she wrote portentously: "[W]e are very unhappy with the [Legislative] Assembly, which demonstrates a softness that would lead us to ruin if the people and the departments did not rise up once more.... The king will toy with us until he has lost us. He preaches the Constitution like the Abby Maury preached religion, mocking it in his heart. I do not presume to be able to resolve the question, but, in faith, here is an adage from Maury that I apply to the current situation: If you want the ends, you must accept the means."[39]

But that was only the beginning of her observations. The events of the morning of August 10 continued:

> Day of blood, day of carnage, and yet day of victory that is doused with our tears. Listen and tremble. The night passed without event; curiosity attracted many people in the faubourgs. That is why they filled the Tuileries with National Guardsmen. The Assembly also had a triple guard. The king, in the morning, reviewed the Swiss troops, around six o'clock. At eight o'clock he went to the National Assembly. The Marseillais joined the Parisian guards fraternally. We heard cries of "long live the king, to hell with the nation," covered by a thousand cries of "long live the Nation." All of a sudden the windows of the chateau were full of Swiss. From every corner, suddenly, they fired on the National Guard. The doors of the chateau opened and shook with canons and revealed a flank facing the people.... The Swiss atoned for their treason by all manner of death. The royal family sought refuge in the Senate. In a favorable moment, they put them in the tribune where they are still.... It was today, the memorable August 10, when the counterrevolution exploded in Paris.[40]

The "second revolution" had begun at daybreak on August 10, when militants captured arms from the Arsenal and overtook the city hall. They convinced the National Guardsmen to join them, and the royal family took refuge in the Legislative Assembly. It was still morning. Once the royal family had evacuated the palace, however, the Swiss and noble troops opened fire on the people. Two hours of killing ensued— "all manner of deaths," as Rosalie explained. Some noble guardsmen were arrested. The focus of the fuselage, however, was the Swiss, who nearly all perished.

Rosalie was elated. She believed that the king had indeed been in league with foreign plotters. She therefore continued, "People of France, you vanquished, in Paris, the Austrian and the Prussian." At the end of the day, she reported, "All afternoon I walked around with Auguste, to the city hall and the palace," demonstrating confidence that she would be safe after the morning battle finished. She had such confidence in the people of Paris that she told Jules, "I am lying down tonight, my door open, even while all of the business owners in the capital put a double lock on their doors in anticipation of brigands." She felt secure despite the fact that "there were two popular executions," referring to noble leaders of the National Guard whose assassinations marked the beginning of combat. Those executions "signaled the awakening of a lion." Rosalie "cover[ed] them with a veil." She told Marc-Antoine, "My sensitive heart cannot stand the image. However, my reason tells me strongly, humanity lost fewer men by the crude barbarity of the people than by the civilized treachery of the King."[41] Her faith in the people to use their power justly was remarkable.

That flutter of her heart aside, Rosalie was overjoyed by the show of force the people exhibited on August 10, as well as the actions that followed. The consequences, she wrote, were that the Feuillants and moderates were effectively discredited. The *journée* saved the Constitution from destruction in their hands. About the letters she wrote to describe August 10, she told Jules, "I wrote a book of observations that assure me of the liberty and glory of my country!"[42] She dated her next letter, as usual, "fourth year of liberty," but now she added, "first year of equality."[43] She contrasted the August 10 demonstration with the Champ de Mars Massacre that had occurred in July 1791, when National Guardsmen fired on protesters who disagreed with the Constituent Assembly's decision to absolve the king for his flight. The comparison was an effective one for Rosalie, who sympathized with the protesters in both events.[44]

Even the calm that followed the event was different, she wrote. "I cannot tell you enough how calm, sure, and tranquil the capital is. It is not from degradation like the day after Champ de Mars, [the memory of which] will never leave my head or heart."[45] She basked in the peaceful and optimistic environment, traversing the Seine in search of happy scenes. "I have never walked as much as I have done since Friday," she told Jules.[46] The relief that she felt after the successful *journée* was magnified by the degree to which it reversed her frustration over the first half of the year, epitomized by the Legislative Assembly's weakness following June 20.

Rosalie credited the August 10 triumph to the people of Paris, the *peuple*, and her respect for them reached a fevered pitch. On August 7, she had been certain that an "explosion" was imminent, and she blamed this tension on the Legislative Assembly's inaction.[47] The next day she had elaborated to Jules, "The [Legislative] Assembly seems to me to be too weak to second the voice of the people, and the people seem too strong to be tamed by the Assembly."[48] If the Assembly was too weak to balance the power of the executive, who was perhaps arming himself against the nation with the support of foreign armies, then the people would provide the bulwark against invasion. In honor of this role, she adorned the people with flowers of praise. "If there are virtues on earth, we must look for them in the rags of the sansculottes," she told Jules.[49] She believed their triumph on August 10 was a sign that "the Supreme Being" was on their side, a belief that also, as she put it, helped her "breathe" for the first time in three years.[50] She now often described the peaceful and virtuous characteristics of the sansculottes, perhaps as a counterpoint to their violence as well as a justification for their exercise of power. On August 27, she went to the Tuileries to witness a memorial for those who perished on August 10, and she explained how impressed she was by the order and peacefulness of the crowd.[51]

An event that took place the night of August 29 makes this point more strongly. Preceding the September Massacres, August 29 was a symptom of the widespread fear of conspiracy. Fifty thousand people took to the streets in search of weapons in others' homes. They meant to disarm any "aristocrat" who might be hiding. They came to Rosalie's apartment. She said she was prepared for them, and she planned to offer Marc-Antoine's rifle immediately, as a show of patriotism and to prevent feeling like a criminal whose weapon was removed by force. The men who came to her door refused to take the rifle, and in fact they stayed for a while to talk about their mutual love for the Revolution. When she asked them not to disturb her elderly neighbor, they agreed. They must have stayed to chat for quite a while, long enough to settle into the apartment and put their things down, because the next day, one of the men returned to retrieve the umbrella he had left at her home.[52]

Not surprisingly, as Rosalie's admiration for the common people grew, her anger against the king increased. Her words grew fiercer when she described the king and his "criminal family." They do not have souls, she told Jules, because they continue to eat and live as if they were unaware of the loss of life on August 10. She, on the other hand, had had difficulty eating.[53] Louis became "Louis the last" in her letters.[54] She told her son in England to be mindful of his surroundings "because wherever there are kings, free men must tremble."[55] Certainly her intolerance of aristocrats also grew. She wished for another revolution, of the August 10 variety, in a couple of years that would oust the aristocrats once and for all.[56]

The *journées* of June 20 and August 10 resulted in vastly different emotions for Rosalie, who was by this point a bona fide Montagnard. The disappointment she felt after June 20 made her distrust the Legislative Assembly and hate the king, while the success of August 10 made her love the people and laid the groundwork for her to accept another, more diabolical bloodletting the following month. The September Massacres began on September 2. Vigilante groups of sansculottes invaded prisons in Paris, organized mock trials for the prisoners, and executed some thirteen hundred of them. They claimed that the prisoners were counterrevolutionaries or "brigands" in the pay of counterrevolutionaries. A majority of the prisoners were priests who had not sworn the oath to the Civil Constitution of the Clergy.

Rosalie had been enjoying supper at a friend's house on September 2. With her was a young Italian man, Bosselini, who was Jules's roommate in London. Rosalie had greeted him warmly through her letters to Jules and assured him that he had "two mothers, one in France."[57] At her invitation, he spent a few weeks with Rosalie; he had just arrived on the first of the month. When they left her friend's house after supper that evening, the streets were teeming. To Marc-Antoine, she described what ensued later that night. While at dinner, she heard cries, "To arms!" "The people said, 'We are leaving our wives and children at home in the middle of our enemies—let us purge them from the earth.'" Outside, she saw "Heads cut off, priests massacred." She, Marion, Bosselini, Auguste, and their host at supper, Monsieur Le Roux, went to the Tuileries and stayed for two hours watching the "groups, women, children, a world, a universe." Growing nervous, they took a carriage home, and during the ride they noticed from Saint-Eustache all the way home that the streets were filled. Upon arriving home, Rosalie found two female friends "taking refuge" at her house, afraid that the presence of "aristocrats" in their own neighborhood would bring trouble.[58]

The next morning, she learned what had taken place. The small church on her street was being demolished (she complained often about the dust), and masons were there most days working on the project. She talked to six of them, and they told her how the crowds had gone to each prison and selected their victims. She wrote to Marc-Antoine, "This new operation of a terrible justice took place under an extraordinary calm. The priests—I silence myself. They were sacrificed to popular vengeance. These masons saw piles of cadavers in the doors of the prisons." She sensed that the masons regretted having been "forced to go along," and she also deplored "the way the culpable and the unlucky innocents [in the prisons] were confused." But she added, "God, have pity on a people who was provoked and led down this path of carnage. Do not punish them."[59]

She did not mention what the young foreigner thought of this unexpected eruption of violence. However, she did continue to report the news her masons told her, and she discussed her support for the people despite the sorrow caused by the bloodshed. "My sensitivity prohibits me from telling you all," she told her husband, "but my reason tells me, 'the Prussians and kings would have done much worse.'" She claimed again and again that the people were forced to commit the crimes, forced "by all those who victimized them for three sad years [since the beginning of the Revolution]."[60] In fact, on September 3 she told Marc-Antoine that some prisoners had been well treated by the vigilantes, and that as she wrote, Paris was again calm. The Massacres were still under way, however, and continued through September 5. She had not yet written to

Jules, likely sensing that this event should not be shared with the English. Eventually she assured Jules, on September 6, that she was well aware of events because "I have my masons who give me reports every morning on the previous night's activities. One of them followed everything without taking part because he is full of humanity and good sense."[61]

Her claim that there was a sense of calm on September 3 is curious. Indeed, she described her own feelings with contradictory images of crisis and peace. "One is astonished, in such crises, to be able to enjoy a perfect repose that is only troubled by the torment of sensitive hearts and tender imaginations aching strangely over the contemplation of so many deaths," she explained to her husband on September 3.[62] How calm could she truly have felt in the wake of massacre? Perhaps her faith in the wisdom of the people helped her ignore the bloodshed that used to trouble her so. That trust likely combined with her fear of foreign plots and conspiracies to assure her that inaction would have been worse.[63]

The priests' martyrdom adds yet another puzzling dimension to Rosalie's acceptance of the Massacres. Throughout the Revolution, she continued to be devout. She believed God was actively involved in the Revolution. Whenever the Revolution achieved a victory, she credited God; whenever it needed help, she assured her correspondents that heaven was preparing a miracle.[64] "Heaven itself is in arms," she said when France entered war with Austria.[65] On August 10, God saved the people from harm, she declared.[66] Rosalie still regretted that the nonjuring priests caused division among the French; she wished that they would embrace the Revolution. This attitude was political, not theological. She even thought that God disliked the rebellious priests. When they demonstrated one day in June, God brought a "deluge of rain" onto their heads, she believed.[67] But a soggy head was different from a bloody one. That same month, Rosalie told Jules about her new friendship with Father Baral, who was apparently a refractory priest. She told Jules that she greatly regretted the hostility directed toward the priests and that it was better to accept differences of opinion than to compel people to change their beliefs.[68] After the Massacres, rather than reconcile her respect for the men of the cloth with her support for the *peuple,* she "silenced" herself altogether.

Rosalie's reaction to the September Massacres evidences how far she allowed her ideological commitment to the sovereignty of the *peuple* to blind her to the violence they committed. Rosalie had warned earlier that to want the ends, they had to accept the means; in September she claimed that virtue could result through violence. In part, this position was made possible by the frightening contexts of foreign war and domestic disunity. It is also critical that her letters to Jules and Marc-Antoine were likely to be circulated beyond her relatives, and her rhetoric was therefore measured. Most important, Rosalie's and Marc-Antoine's allegiance to the extreme Left, the Mountain, was decisive in her commentary on the Massacres. On the eve of August 10, the Left was in the process of dividing. One major element in the divergence of the Montagnards and the Girondins was the groups' different reactions to the September Massacres. The Girondins were suspicious of popular uprisings; the Montagnards constantly supported the sansculottes. For the Montagnards, the presupposition that the "voice of the people was the voice of God" led to a necessary acceptance, at least in rhetoric, of their actions.

The Julliens' alliance with the Mountain was especially clear when Marc-Antoine was elected a member of the National Convention, the political body that succeeded the Legislative Assembly on September 20. Marc-Antoine was a representative of the Drôme; he returned to Paris to begin his job. He spoke infrequently, but when he did, he clearly asserted his Montagnard position. On October 18, the secretary at the Convention had just read a letter from one of the Parisian sections that asked the Convention for money to provide basic sustenance to the indigent in Paris. Another member of the Convention said it was unacceptable to use national funds for Parisians, as the Convention had already decided when the women of Les Halles asked for money the day before. He moved to turn to the order of the day.

Marc-Antoine interrupted, however, and persisted for several minutes in the face of "many murmurs" and shouts of "*à l'ordre!*" to contend that the Convention had to take this request seriously. "Monsieurs," he said, "we are the representatives of the poor. We are the fathers of the *peuple* who have long been victims of the rich. We owe them our help." He moved from his seat to the middle of the hall. "We have given the *peuple* immense political rights, but not to plunge them into misery!" After more interruptions, he exclaimed, "I should be heard in an assembly where one can find all the talents, patriotism, and virtues of a Republic. I speak in the name of the *peuple*. I do not deserve to be seen as an agitator. I have proven my good citizenship. I have constantly defended the *peuple*'s cause. I have lived in obscurity. I understand all the *peuple*'s troubles. And I resolved to extinguish the source of those troubles." The spectators in the tribunes applauded, but the Convention members convinced him to sit down so they could pass to the order of the day.[69]

Marc-Antoine concluded quickly by suggesting that the Convention could easily find the funds necessary to support the impoverished Parisians by reallocating the wealth of "the rich bankers, financiers, [and] aristocratic notaries who only paid a quarter of their patriotic contribution."[70] He asserted his position as a Montagnard by supporting the people of Paris and by identifying himself not as a wealthy banker but as an "obscure" person of the people.[71] The antagonism Rosalie and Marc-Antoine had felt in the 1780s toward the wealthy financiers informed their political opinions as some members of the Left pushed for greater and greater economic equality.

Rosalie could not become a member of the Convention, and yet her disenfranchisement did not prevent her from developing a political consciousness or from feeling connected to revolutionary culture. Her political identity ripened in the summer of 1792 as a result of her participation in three activities: attending events, debating with friends, and frequent letter writing.

Because Rosalie was no longer frightened by the passions in the Assembly or the protests in Paris, she began to witness events about which she had much to say. After Jules left for London, Rosalie began to meet often with friends. A mostly female group of friends and relatives met once a week for an afternoon meal that usually ended around five o'clock. The women read letters aloud, discussed current events, and then went from dinner to the Legislative Assembly or a patriotic festival. Sometimes they invited important men to join them, as they did once in April. Rosalie told Marc-Antoine that at this dinner, there were "vigorous patriots present: [a] commander of a battalion, a captain, and a brave soldier from Châteauvieux who told us very interesting stories."[72] The Swiss soldiers of Châteauvieux had just gained amnesty for the offense of failing to obey orders from an aristocrat in 1790. Rosalie had attended a festival on the Champ de Mars that honored them two weeks before this dinner. It is no wonder that she was excited to talk with one of the soldiers, as she too saw herself as a "vigorous patriot."

As a result of witnessing important events and discussing them with friends, Rosalie had a lot of content for her letters to Marc-Antoine and Jules, who were in Romans and London and needed her updates. Her two audiences required different types of letters. She told Jules on two occasions that she worried about her letters being intercepted in London. She told him she would be "circumspect" and not "too patriotic" in case they landed in the wrong hands.[73] In addition to that caution, however, Rosalie wrote carefully so that her writing *would* be read widely. As her son mingled with people such as Stanhope, he could use her letters to give the English news directly from his mother in the middle of Paris. She assured her readers on June 1, "I am more exact than a journalist."[74] Through her son, Rosalie became an ambassador of the Revolution.

In turn, Jules told her about England, which she found fascinating. She asked him many questions: What do the English think of our revolution? Is it true that the British are winning a battle in the Indian Kingdom of Mysore? How do the English treat their slaves?[75] Have you met any Quakers? Did Voltaire describe the Quakers accurately? If you see one, greet him for me. In short, "I read everything about England. I am half English."[76] His reports on Englishmen's personalities were not flattering. "You are among a cold and pensive people," she responded in May.[77] In June she advised him, "Defend yourself against the dark English 'humor.'"[78]

He wanted to come home, but she tried to give him the fortitude to carry out his term. She told him about little details from home. Auguste gave a short speech at the Jacobin Club and was warmly received by the Mountain.[79] He got a little bird as a pet, a bullfinch. "Your brother is crazy about him."[80] She kept him engaged in his environment by asking questions about England. She told him he was becoming a man of virtue, that she was so proud of him. "I only know one lasting beauty. I only know one solid good, one path to true glory. It is virtue. All the rest is illusory," she wrote encouragingly in May.[81] As she thought about his virtue, his patriotism, and his potential in the New Regime, she wrote on August 25, "My happiness, joy, and glory lies in you."[82]

Through Marc-Antoine, Rosalie addressed a different audience: like-minded Jacobins. She wrote to him about events and her reactions to engage in conversation the way she conversed with friends at dinner. She wrote in the language of the Left, expressing solidarity with the Mountain and welcoming responses. She called Marc-Antoine her "reading light" and asked him constantly for his opinion.[83] "Events are happening so rapidly, so astonishingly, so bizarrely, it's mind boggling. Where are you?" she asked as she began her description of June 20.[84] His letters to her are not in the archives, but they surely helped her refine her thoughts as she processed her surroundings.

All of these changes in Rosalie's public life also altered her personal life, especially her family dynamics and her identity as a woman.[85] The personal and the political were already blended together in the Revolution. The revolutionaries knew that to promote equality in society, they had to begin at home by reducing the force of patriarchy and making the family into a miniature republic. In 1792, the government made marriage a civil contract and legalized divorce to allow unhappy families to disband and seek the domestic happiness that would engender good patriotism. Rosalie joked about the new law. She wrote to her husband on August 30, "Divorce is decreed, or soon will be. You no longer have a wife."[86] She quickly clarified her levity on September 1: "I send you kisses from the bottom of my heart, and I am your wife."[87] The loving sentiment was all the more meaningful now that the longevity of their marriage was their choice.

In other ways, Rosalie wrote about her evolving place within the family. In 1792, she wrote to Marc-Antoine as she sometimes had done in the Old Regime, reverently praising his virtue and his leadership in the home. But just as her apologies to patriarchy had been at least a little rhetorical in the Old Regime, they were nearly farcical in the Revolution. She wrote to Marc-Antoine one day about his brother Bernard's offer to take care of Auguste so that she could go to the Legislative Assembly. She claimed that she did not shirk her maternal responsibilities despite her brother-in-law's suggestion because "I know how to control myself. . . . I would rather sacrifice a truly grand pleasure and stay at my post." She said that she decided to stay home because "the first question of [her] heart" was whether or not Marc-Antoine would approve.[88]

This anecdote is strange because very little ever prevented Rosalie from going to the Assembly or other meetings and events. If Marion and Auguste did not go with her, then Auguste stayed behind with Marion. Rosalie continued by writing that she respected Marc-Antoine's wishes because nature made the two sexes differently. "Your principles are firmer, your outlook more far-reaching, your wisdom more male," she explained. "But I am equal to you in my love of true, beautiful morality, and I would not love you so much and so constantly and for so long if you had not developed, before my eyes, all of these characteristics. It is love of virtue that inspires my love for Monsieur Jullien."[89] As she wrote this letter in April, the possibility of divorce was not yet an issue. But in a regime that was dismantling hierarchies, Rosalie emphasized the contractual nature of her marriage and depicted herself as a woman free to choose a virtuous spouse.

She was also beginning to develop a public identity that extended beyond her familial identity. Her description of herself as a journalist is one indication that her "profession" was a new, important component of her sense of self. She assumed a political identity through her own efforts, not simply through her relationship to an active citizen. As the Revolution, and Rosalie, became more radical in the following year, her sense of womanhood would change even more.

The events of June 20, August 10, and September 2–5 changed the nature of the Revolution forever, culminating in the declaration of the First Republic on September 22. Throughout this pivotal year,

Rosalie developed a political ideology that developed far beyond her Old Regime worldview, encouraged by unforeseen *journées*. Her old values—family, religion, modesty, and industriousness—assumed new meaning in 1792. The national family should be unified; the Revolution was God's will; the humbler the person, the more virtuous he was; and service to the nation was the hallmark of patriotism. When these values became extreme, such as during the September Massacres, the continuity with her Old Regime worldview halted, and the reaction to new circumstances began.

As Rosalie's political ideology became clearer, her political identity also took shape. For the first time, she saw herself as a revolutionary not because of her intellectual support of the Revolution, but because of her involvement in the revolutionary process. Because of meaningful interactions with other revolutionaries, whether in Paris, the provinces, or London, she had a role to play in the Revolution. Although she did not participate in the violence of the *journées*, she did act by watching them unfold and sharing her observations and commentaries with Jules, Marc-Antoine, and her extended readership in London and Romans. Her political life began to penetrate deeply into her sense of self. She told Virginie the night before the August 10 revolution, "The affairs of the state are the affairs of my heart. I do not think, dream, or feel anything but that, my child."[90]

Coincidentally, Rosalie's previous interpretation of the Revolution as a slow and inevitable process also changed in 1792. Whereas earlier she was confident that humankind would eventually evolve into "real republicans," suddenly in 1792 she declared the process finished. By October, she was certain that the metamorphosis into republicans had taken place in everyone. "We do not seem like a menaced or beaten people, but a great and jubilant family. If anyone thinks otherwise, he does not know the new Frenchman," she told Jules triumphantly.[91] How did this change come about? As she wrote, "Circumstances make the man."[92] Similarly, Rosalie's extensive experience in the historic events of 1792 turned this passive citizen into an active revolutionary.

5

Adopting the Terror

AFTER RETURNING FROM London at the end of 1792, Jules sought
a new job. As luck would have it, the brother of Marc-Antoine's old
friend and Rousseau sparring mate, Joseph Servan, was minister of war.
He gave Jules a position as assistant war commissioner.[1] Jules's duties
included recruiting troops, which he did with measurable success. One
of his first destinations was the Pyrenees, where he visited a town called
Tarbes. With her son now working more directly for the government,
Rosalie developed a sense of her relationship to the state that was much
more personal. She wrote to Jules, "My soul lives in Tarbes, Monsieur le
Commissaire, and my gratitude for this small corner of the world makes
it my adoptive hometown."[2] Her choice of words here is intriguing.

In a Revolution where fraternity was a founding ideal, the image of
the nation as family permeated revolutionary culture. Speaking about
the country in family terms was not new; the king had often been discussed in the language of paternalism.[3] During the Revolution, metaphors of family abounded. When émigrés departed, they were called
disobedient children who ran away from their mother country. On the
other hand, others could be "adopted" by the mother. If a French woman
married a foreigner, for example, the law stated that he was "adopted"
by the French nation and given French citizenship. In a famous case, a
young woman named Suzanne Lepeltier lost her father to an assassin
in 1793 after he voted for the king's execution. The government then
"adopted" Suzanne in a public ceremony.[4]

Rosalie's "adoption" of Tarbes as her hometown built on the preva-
lent symbolism of the family. But it is also easy to mix metaphors. Rosalie
had real kin who were becoming inheritors of the Revolution. With her

son an agent of the state, Rosalie became a matriarch of greater propor-
tions. Her feeling of natural, maternal obligation to her son's associates
was an important component of her acceptance of terrorist policies in
Year II. Just as she "adopted" Tarbes because it had welcomed her son,
she felt akin to Jules's Jacobin "brothers" in government. She adopted
them and the policies they crafted, including the Terror.

The Terror was the nearly yearlong period of suspension of civil
rights and execution of alleged counterrevolutionaries that began in
the fall of 1793 (the beginning of Year II of the French revolutionary
calendar) and ended in the summer of 1794. The Terror commenced on
September 17, 1793, with the Law of Suspects, which allowed the arrest
of anyone who appeared unpatriotic. Nobles, hoarders, and émigrés
were obvious targets, but the interpretation of counterrevolutionary
activity was subjective. The events that led to this climax were complex.
In the background were layers of anxieties, caused by real and imagined
threats. The real threats were unavoidable: war with Austria and Prussia
was going poorly, counterrevolutionaries took up arms in the Vendée,
and the cost of food threatened to make life impossible for many. On
the other hand, the fear of conspiracies was perhaps more insidious
because it was less easy to contain.

Rumors of plots against the revolutionary government were at least
as old as May 1792, when Brissot and Gensonné announced that an
Austrian committee was scheming to destroy the Revolution. Panic
spread among the assemblymen and quickly infected the rest of Paris,
whose sansculottes patrolled the streets with weapons. From that
point, the Paris sections were, as Hanson notes, "in a state of declared
insurrection."[5] The fear of conspiracies continued through the summer
of 1794. Radical Jacobins were most likely to become conspiracy theorists, perhaps because of their belief that they possessed the truest understanding of democracy. Tackett concludes, "It was only one step further
to the assumption that all who disagreed with the Jacobins' positions
must of necessity be fools, dupes, or conspirators."[6] The rumors that the
Jacobins and others entertained and the real threats facing France all
combined to create a culture of fear.[7]

In that environment, disagreements between deputies took a lethal turn, as the Girondins would soon learn. Hanson describes three fundamental ideological divergences between the Girondins and the Montagnards: the use of violence, the nature of sovereignty, and the leadership of Paris in national politics. The Girondins were less inclined to support popular violence, especially from the people of Paris. The Montagnards, on the other hand, identified themselves as true representatives of the *peuple*. Thus the Jacobins emphasized the general will, while the Girondins were wary of the power wielded by the Parisian sections and Paris's dominance in revolutionary politics.[8] The Julliens adhered to the Mountain. Not only did Marc-Antoine speak on behalf of the sansculottes in 1792, but he also sided with the Mountain during Louis XVI's trial. He was one of the small majority who voted for the king's execution, which took place on January 21, 1793. Rosalie agreed with her husband's vote, writing in the spring of 1793 that she supported the Mountain precisely because it replaced the king's sovereignty with the rule of law.[9]

The schism between the Girondin and Jacobin deputies was dramatic on a personal level. Just as friendship had been a serious institution in the Old Regime, entailing conventions of obligation and loyalty, it was also heavy with meaning during the Revolution. Friendship "formed an integral part" of politics in the Republic. And yet, as Linton notes, the Jacobins had an "ambiguous attitude toward friendship," valuing it as a basis of civil society on one hand and being wary of "false friends" on the other.[10] They feared that friendship networks could conceal conspiracies. Robespierre even accused the Girondins of being friends with the treasonous General Dumouriez in place of finding real evidence that they had conspired with him.[11] Robespierre held only a small circle of friends once he entered the Committee of Public Safety. Rosalie was among the elite in that regard. Her allegiance to the Mountain was not only ideological but also personal.

Friendships helped ensure that Rosalie would join the Mountain. First, she and Marc-Antoine became familiar with Bertrand Barère in the spring and summer of 1793. In April, when Jules was in Barère's hometown, she told Jules that "Barère had often spoken to your father [about Tarbes] with affection."[12] In April and May, they had dinner together on several occasions.[13] On May 19, she wrote Jules: "I had dinner with Barère on Friday, and he assured me that he only had honorable and good news from Tarbes." Then she communicated that Barère agreed that factionalism in politics "places us at an abyss as profound as the one created by the ruses of the aristocracy. He maintains that every exaggeration is evil and that we must moderate the malicious who want good through violent means. He is like Fabius the temporizer."[14] Barère, whom Rosalie likened to a Roman statesman, provide her with dialogue and insight into revolutionary politics. Like the other Montagnards, he claimed to stand for unity.

If the Mountain believed in unity, then their opponents stood for conflict. This was how Rosalie now viewed her former friends in the Girondin party. In May 1793, when tension between the groups was at its peak, Rosalie went constantly to the Convention. She told Jules on May 2, "Yesterday and the day before, I sat in the benches of the Senate from ten o'clock in the morning until seven o'clock at night. All I had for provisions was a roll and some squares of chocolate."[15] On May 14, she warned that the Girondin party would "ruin patriotism completely in this great city." Without "the active surveillance of Parisians, there would be a deadly preponderance of this terrible party, and it would destroy the Republic by reversing the Mountain."[16] On May 28, she recounted that she had again spent all day at the Convention, throughout its fourteen-hour session. "I was there, my friend. I would write a letter of fourteen pages if I were to tell you the infinite details of this important day."[17] The day was one during which the Committee of Twelve was suspended. The committee had been a Girondin bulwark against the people of Paris and had been arresting people suspected of vigilantism. The Montagnard position opposed the "tyranny of the Committee of Twelve," as Rosalie described it in the same letter.

The curtain was setting on the Girondins throughout that month. On June 2, the Girondin deputies were arrested. By June 10, the Montagnards were in control of the Committee of Public Safety.

The Jacobins soon adopted a new constitution that granted universal male suffrage and confirmed that the people were the source of sovereignty. When the Constitution was brought before the Convention, Rosalie "lived at the Senate for three days straight." Participation in this historic event touched her deeply. She explained: "Paris presents, these days, the most beautiful spectacle in the history of men. I would like to paint it like Tacitus [the ancient Roman historian], if only I knew where to find his brush. Alas, my dear friend, as I only have my plume…"[18] Rosalie was constantly at the Convention that summer. When Marc-Antoine was ill in July, she went vigilantly to take notes for him. She wrote to Jules about it: "I am the supplement to my legislator. I go everyday to the Assembly to give him an account."[19] This job gave her a political role that was different from any she had yet experienced.

At this point, her friendship with Robespierre grew. The Julliens were acquainted with Robespierre first through the Jacobin Club. Rosalie also knew of him through his speeches and journal publications. As early as August 1791, she added his name to her list of beloved revolutionaries.[20] She was confident that Robespierre embodied the traits that she valued. "Robespierre is a man who is devoted to the public with the generosity of the greatest men of Antiquity," she told Marc-Antoine in the summer of 1792.[21] She echoed the sentiment a few days later, writing, "This Robespierre is a real Roman."[22]

Rosalie's friendship with Robespierre deepened over the course of the next year. Following the drafting of the new Constitution, Rosalie and Marc-Antoine had dinner with Barère and Robespierre. Rosalie wrote to Jules about it: "It was the happy day of the end of the discussion of the Social Contract [the 1793 Constitution]. It was seven in the evening when we sat down at the table, and our guests were famished but filled with glory because Barère and Robespierre had spoken with so much justice and eloquence that both of them received the most sincere applause. I said what was in my heart and we drank to [your] health." The personal satisfaction that she took in her friends' success, her maternal pride over these leaders' respect for her son, and her philosophical appreciation of politics that she interpreted in Rousseau's democratic language all combined to feed her sense of hope and optimism in the summer of 1793. She concluded the letter, "We must see each other often to feed the sweet fraternity that must reunite all real Republicans."[23] And they did, five days later.[24] Six months after that, Robespierre was the host. "I dined last night at Robespierre's house, and as we were seated next to each other, we spoke about you—to the extent that his terseness allowed."[25] Perhaps this terseness is the reason Rosalie provides few insights into Robespierre's character. However, her respect for his principles is clear. Not only was Rosalie attracted to the Montagnards' ideology, but she was also personally attached to the group's members. As she told Jules in December 1793, "The Committee of Public Safety [is] composed of men whom I esteem because of my familiarity with each one."[26]

Jean-Paul Marat was a different story. "His heart is pure, but his head is too exalted," she explained.[27] But she also declared that the Girondins had created a Marat figure that was more menacing than the real man.[28] Indeed, she found the real Marat laughable and maintained that he did not represent the Mountain. She wrote to Jules soon after Marat had been exonerated of Girondin accusations in May:

> Marat is not powerful in the Mountain or among the *peuple*; it is a lie to make him appear in the departments as if he is the leader of the party. For us he is the lunatic of the Revolution and the craziest of patriots. Sometimes he says excellent things, and we believe he has a good heart, pure soul, and an outlook that is revolutionary, helpful, and profound. We approve when he says good things; we laugh at his fits that are no more dangerous for the Republic than a child's tantrum is for his nurse. If you saw him lounging or fidgeting around the Senate, you would laugh with all your heart.[29]

Marat was so harmless, in her eyes, that she believed any fear of him must have been inspired by Girondin lies.

In fact, once Charlotte Corday assassinated Marat on July 13, Rosalie believed that Corday was the "passive instrument" of the

Girondins. After the event, Rosalie wrote to a contact in the Drôme so that the truth might be reported there. She explained that Corday had "plunged her homicidal dagger into the chest of *Marat Fantastique*," the imaginary Marat the Girondins had created to frighten the people.[30] To her, his assassination was proof that the aristocrats and Girondins were spreading lies about Marat and the Mountain throughout the provinces. She did not mourn Marat, but she lamented the division Girondins were causing throughout the country. The letter was read aloud in Valence, and it was received by "applause" for "enlightened, sensible, and intrepid patriotism."[31]

Rosalie's way with words was an asset to her family. Her requests for letters for Jules's trip to London had been amply met. When he needed a new occupation after traveling with the army, his parents' friends proved helpful. In September he became, as Palmer describes, "a kind of special agent, or traveling inspector, for the Committee of Public Safety."[32] Palmer suggests that a speech Jules gave in January 1792 at the Jacobin Club caught Robespierre's eye and helped him get the job.[33] Surely the topic also came up at dinner one day at Rosalie's home. Rosalie and Marc-Antoine were also recruited into service when Jules received this position. It was decided that Jules would send all of his correspondence intended for the committee to his parents. Either Rosalie or Marc-Antoine carried the letters by hand to the intended recipients.[34]

The Committee of Public Safety was not mistaken in selecting Jules for the task. He was committed to the Revolution, the committee, and his job. Just as he was required, he wrote many letters to the committee. Enemies would later accuse Jules of being Robespierre's crony, but his defenders countered that Jules wrote to all members of the committee and was transparent in all of his official business.[35] In turn, the committee admired what they called his "mild manner and republican energy."[36] His tasks were to report on the state of patriotism wherever he went and to ensure the capture of Girondins who had fled Paris.

A letter from a different hand stands out in the archive at this moment. It was addressed to Rosalie from Saint-Cyr Nugues, who seems to have gotten over his argument with her from two years earlier.

He wrote warmly, "I learned, *citoyenne*, from a short letter from [Jules] Jullien that he is leaving now on mission for the Committee of Public Safety for the principal cities of the realm. Thus he has left for his destiny, an errant and uncertain life." He praised Jules for throwing himself into a public career, "that he might march to glory." He was impressed that "on the first try, he attained a height that would frighten most people. But for him it was only encouraging. What joy you must be feeling, tender and lovable mother." Saint-Cyr was especially impressed because he had not been as successful at finding a job thus far. He asked Rosalie if she might put in a good word for him among "your acquaintances in the Assembly." He signed his letter, "Your son."[37] The Julliens were not able to help him find a job, but Saint-Cyr's career needed no assistance after all. His name is now among those of the other generals who were the first to be listed on the Arc de Triomphe.

Jules's mission took him to several cities in Brittany in the fall, before he turned south to Nantes in January, La Rochelle in February, and finally Bordeaux in April. Rosalie followed him with interest. As before, she consoled him along the way as well. When his trunk was delayed on its journey to him in Brest, she joked, "Since you are the apostle of sansculottism, be *sans-culottes* [without breaches]. Lead by example. Simplicity accompanies equality."[38] At other times, Rosalie was more serious. Two such instances were when officials in La Rochelle briefly imprisoned Jules after a power struggle and when Jean-Lambert Tallien and Claude-Alexandre Ysabeau, who had been sent as representatives on mission in September, similarly bristled at Jules's arrival.

Levity was also infrequent in her letters because Jules visited some of the most troubling examples of revolutionary violence. He reached Nantes on January 29, 1794. The month before, one of the most gruesome episodes of the Terror had concluded. Under the direction of Jean-Baptiste Carrier, a representative on mission, boatloads of prisoners were taken into the Loire and drowned. As many as two thousand men, women, and children were killed this way, without trials and with particular cruelty. Jules wrote to the Committee of Public Safety about the *noyades* on February 3: "I am assured that he had all those who filled the prisons at Nantes taken out indiscriminately, put on boats, and sunk in the Loire. He told me to my face that that was the only way to run a revolution, and he called Prieur of the Marne [the previous, less violent representative] a fool for thinking of nothing to do with suspects except confine them."[39] The committee recalled Carrier.

Rosalie was the first to read Jules's complaint and to respond to him about Carrier and his recall. The letter is worth reproducing at length because it illustrates her relationship with Jules as well as her rhetoric of confidence in the government at this time.

Dear friend, I am the one who will respond to you, and I second your impatience. The deputy from Nantes is recalled, and they are sending brave Prieur [de la Marne] in his place.... The abuse of power is angering and [yet] natural during this moment of crisis because power is in so many incapable hands that it is bound to give rise to mistakes of every sort. My blood boils in my veins, thinking about all of the bad that comes of doing good. Patience and courage. The instrument will perfect itself. Vice works for the profit of virtue. Your father saw Robespierre, who read your letter carefully. He asked your father to tell you how happy he was with your operations and your perspective, which is useful. Barère asked St-Cyr [Nugues] to research all of your letters and to present an analysis to him.... When you do not know what to do, rely on your good speculations and give them confidently to the Committee of Public Safety. There they are only concerned with the general good, and if the amount of business they deal with prevents them from responding quickly, that does not mean they lack zeal, and you must not doubt that you are one of the agents with whom they have the most communication and for whom they have perhaps the most tender consideration, founded on your virtuous republicanism. Robespierre, by virtue of his last discourse, will give luster and confidence to government again. Say to yourself, "That which he says, I will do." This Committee holds treasures of virtues and talents. Robert Lindet, Couthon, Barère, Jean Bon Saint-André, St Just, etc., etc.[40]

Rosalie continued to trust the men she knew and admired. The speech she mentioned was Robespierre's infamous discourse from February 5, in which he connected the ideals of virtue and terror. A well-run republic required a combination of both, he said: "virtue, without which terror is fatal; terror, without which virtue is powerless." In his words, terror responded to "our country's most urgent needs." It was "nothing other than justice, prompt, severe, inflexible." Twelve days after the speech, and six days after the above letter, Rosalie wrote to her son, "Robespierre's discourse is still warm in my soul. He preaches virtue, and I hope he propagates it.... It is the primary necessity, and the only basis of the Republic."[41]

Rosalie's approval of Jacobin policies was certainly influenced by the fact that the authors of those policies were friends. In fact, with Jules an agent of the Committee of Public Safety and Marc-Antoine a secretary of the Jacobin Club beginning in February, Rosalie spent a great deal of her time in their company. She shared meals with them, attended their meetings, and even cared for them when they were frail. The Jacobin Club became ever more like home to Rosalie; the boundary between her political life and her family life all but disappeared.

The physical boundary that separated Rosalie's apartment from the spectacle of the streets was also a critical place. The view afforded by her window attracted a friend in October 1793. The acclaimed painter and politician Jacques-Louis David was also a friend of Robespierre. Rosalie became acquainted with him in the summer of 1793.[42] When Marie-Antoinette was to be carted to the guillotine, Rosalie invited him to her apartment, where he famously sketched the queen.

Rosalie's experience of the Revolution at this point was surely unlike any other's. When her husband was secretary of the Jacobin Club, she attended meetings just as often as he. She wrote to Jules, "Your father is the secretary to the Jacobins, which doubles my fervor. I go to every meeting."[43] She also assumed a nurturing role when Robespierre and Georges Couthon became ill in February. Rosalie saw them often, providing care as well as communication between them and her son. By the end of the month, she was able to report, "Robespierre and Couthon

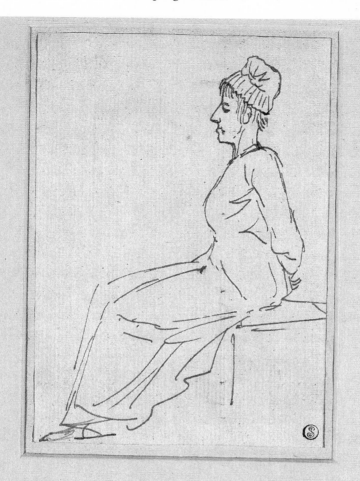

Portrait de marie Antoinette - reine de france conduite au Supplice; dessiné à la plume par David Spectateur du Convoi, & Placé sur la fenetre avec la Citoyenne Jullien épouse du représentant jullien, de qui je tiens Cette piece.

Jacques-Louis David sketched this profile of Marie-Antoinette on her way to the guillotine "from the window of Citoyenne Jullien." Rosalie was acquainted with the painter through the Jacobin Club. Together she and David watched the fallen queen in October 1793. Erich Lessing/Art Resource, NY.

are doing better. I can't begin to convey the tender concerns people are expressing [over their health]. Their recovery will bring joy to all. I go often to the two of them and see them at their homes. They are more exhausted than sick."[44] Rosalie's Jacobin family, which included members of her nuclear family, provided her insight into the Revolution, a closeness to the seat of power she had never known before, and knowledge of the leadership that gave her confidence in their ability to weather the Revolution's troubles and ultimately establish a republic based on virtue.

Her increasing proximity to the Committee of Public Safety resulted in more abundant and better-defined ideology in her letters to Jules. In February, she offered the following conclusion about current events: "I stand behind this thesis: man is good and, in general, reveres virtue. In the flood of our vices, I still collect consoling proofs of virtue." This belief in the basic goodness of man sounds like Rousseau, but it is here that Marc-Antoine's old mentor finally enters her letters. She continued: "The virtues of a free people are so necessary to its liberty that they can only achieve liberty if they conserve their virtue. Domestic virtues lead to public morality; without morals, laws are useless. Voilà: that is pure Mably, taken from [*Entretiens de*] Phocion."[45] This reference was Rosalie's second citation of Mably. The first was in the letter to Jules about Carrier's recall. She wrote, "We are reading the *Entretiens de Phocion*, and I am finding so many things in it that are relevant today. I must tell you at least one: 'Virtue unites men by inspiring mutual confidence. Vice, on the contrary, keeps them on guard against each other and divides them.' Apply this principle, my friend. Virtue is as necessary as bread. Adieu."[46] Rosalie's invocation of Mably was meant to support Robespierre's belief that vice would always seek to divide the nation. That threat must be contained.

Rosalie reread the writings of her old friend Mably, but she also adopted the language of her new friends. In part because she knew her letters had the potential—sometimes intended—to be read aloud and circulated, she became a mouthpiece for the Jacobins. Rosalie justified the Terror by offering examples of justice in the Revolutionary Tribunals. In one instance, she explained that she was glad someone had been acquitted. She knew that he was incapable of doing wrong and was pleased that while the culpable were being punished, the innocent were spared. She then included theoretical justifications for the extermination of counterrevolutionaries. After all, the Terror targeted their enemies, she said. She explained in December 1793 that enemies were abundant, and the new laws were a necessary response to them:

> If all the agents of the Republic [were not] thinly spread throughout the Empire, if all of the public functionaries were touched with great principles of justice, if the red [revolutionary] cap did not sit on the heads of aristocrats who try to extinguish liberty while pretending to embrace it, our new revolutionary laws would be dangerous or ineffectual....But, my friend, laws are only made for troublemakers...Take a glance at our Republic's situation: she is assailed by an exterior enemy, devoured by an interior enemy.[47]

She also added that because only the guilty were affected by the Reign of Terror, a better word than *terror* would be *justice*. She reiterated this idea in February, writing, "Union is the order of the day for republicans as terror is for their enemies. I would like to be able to change this word to justice. Justice has the right effect because justice strikes down criminals and is the terror of wrongdoers."[48]

Rosalie's experience of Year II was not the typical experience for a Parisian woman. In fact, it is remarkable that Rosalie's role in politics increased in this year, because another feature of Year II was a decisive turn against women's political participation. Following a public disturbance by the women of Les Halles, the Convention voted to disband women's political clubs in September. The next few months brought even more restrictions: women's prohibition from participating in political assembly, the request that wives of Convention representatives return to their home provinces, and even the declaration that groups of more than five women together in public could be placed under arrest. Historians largely agree that these laws formed, as Hufton puts it, "an attempt to silence once and for all the engendered crowd."[49]

And yet, because of Rosalie's unique political responsibilities, her sense of womanhood evolved significantly in the radical phase of the Revolution. This process began in the summer, before women were silenced. Rosalie began to speak about women in more active terms while also becoming bolder in her efforts to speak publicly. In June, she wrote a letter to the procurer general of the Drôme and asked that he disseminate her epistle. In it, she described women's task:

> Dear citizen, our politics is founded entirely on morality and vir-tue. If my husband, who emblazoned these traits on the hearts of his two sons and on the soul of his wife, did not practice them with the firmness of a Republican in our eyes, he would no longer have a wife or children. Do not think that these feel-ings are particular to me. They animate all the real Republican *mères de familles*, and I know two thousand in Paris even more emphatic than I in their exclamation of, and pride in, this convic-tion.... They all have husbands and children whom they cherish, whom they correct if they are misguided, whom they denounce when they are corrupt.[50]

In this depiction, not only were mothers active in their support of republican virtues in the home, but also their allegiance to the Republic came first. They were female citizens before they were wives. Women's identities did not rely on their family position, though their position in the family could give them power. Their duty to police the interior of their homes and separate themselves from it if necessary made them independent. The idea of women policing France's interior while the men fought on the battlefield was not original to Rosalie. Although she never joined any official women's clubs, her ideas were similar to those of Pauline Léon, who founded the Society of Republican Revolutionary Women (*citoyennes*) in May 1793, the month before Rosalie wrote to the Drôme.[51] Rosalie had already asserted, that April, "I dare say, there are French women who, though not yet Spartans or Romans, are capable of achieving Republican virtues with less effort than men."[52] Like other women, she believed that women could embody exceptional republican traits.[53]

It is noteworthy that Rosalie made greater efforts to publicize her thoughts at this point. Similar letters addressed to a wider public appeared in July after Marat's assassination. She later wrote to Jules about one of these public letters, explaining that although she usually considered publication to be too immodest for women, she hoped that since "the motives that direct me are so independent of egotism, and the circumstances were so particular, the good Jean-Jacques [Rousseau] himself could change his mind" about the propriety of public speaking.[54] She asserted that she did not doubt the appropriateness of her writing because the Republic was in trouble. In fact, rather than apologize for her gender, in this letter she used it to justify writing. It was important that a good female patriot elevate the morale of the Drômois and inspire the Drômoises to follow her example.

Rosalie's own experience gave her a new outlook, but so did the trend toward greater gender equality in the spring and summer of 1793—before the turn of events in the fall. An official decision in March declared that women's loyalty to the Republic superseded their familial bonds. The law targeted women who emigrated with their spouses and claimed that they had no choice but to obey their husbands. Women who left the country because they followed their husbands were subject to death upon return; thus women were given the responsibility and independence to choose the national family over the conjugal family.[55] That same month, a law requiring equal inheritance among all children added to women's gains in legal equality. In addition, as Godineau notes, "the summer of 1793 was unquestionably the period when militants and authorities accepted women's participation in the popular movement with the most indulgence, and even enthusiasm."[56]

Rosalie witnessed that enthusiasm firsthand. In July, she described how the Parisian sections entered the Convention. One of them was full of women, "beautiful as the Graces...the generous wives of soldiers who are fighting at our frontiers or in the Vendée." And then, "a troop of young boys, the hope of the *patrie.*" The people continued to enter.

"A new section, a new charm. The blind and deaf and mute... gave the most touching and astounding concert." Finally, she announced:

> Awaken your attention again! The multitude of men, women, and children part ways to let a troop of virgin *citoyennes* pass. They carried the national colors and the grace of youth, and came into the middle of the room. "Frenchmen, once lazy, renounce your frivolity! Respect republican modesty! We had the double burden of being the object of your adorations and of your wrongs. Now we only want to be the companions to your virtues and the objects of your esteem. If you have the power to make laws, engrave one in bronze for us. Let it impose on the strong sex respect for the weak one. The regeneration of morals is the only solid base of your magnificent edifice.... We swear to marry only Republicans."

Rosalie went on to recount how the virgins' speech inspired another woman near her. The woman said to her boyfriend, who had abandoned the army fighting the Vendéens, "You were the object of my love, but you have become the object of my contempt. All connection is ruptured between a coward and a real *citoyenne*. Long live the Republic, long live the Mountain!"[57] Not only was Rosalie's patriotism bolstered during this festival, but she also felt particularly emboldened by the strong show of women as participants.

Rosalie's enthusiasm for being present at events such as these must have led to great disappointment for her when women's public assembly was prohibited in the fall of 1793. But because that event coincided with Jules's job with the Committee of Public Safety, Rosalie was less affected by the restrictions than she would have been otherwise. She remained in close contact with the government because of her friendships and her role as secretary to Jules. She mentioned the ban on assembly in only one letter. She told Jules, "The tribunes [of the Convention], where we used to go, inside the hall, are not admitting women anymore. They made them leave on who knows what pretext. It means I cannot attend the sessions." She consoled herself by saying that she preferred being outside the Convention anyway, "because there I can better study public opinion, and there I find myself among my true friends, the sansculottes."[58] Rosalie soon found other outlets for her impulse to be near the epicenter of the Revolution. Her most beloved role was that of mentor to her son.

Rosalie saw her role as Jules's mother assume new responsibilities during his political career. Not only did she transmit his letters to the Committee of Public Safety, but she also kept him abreast of news in the capital and offered him advice and support. Sometimes she was specific in her advice. For example, Rosalie opposed the drastic measures that were being taken toward de-Christianization. The new secular calendar established on September 22, 1792, was particularly insulting to the devout. It divided weeks into ten days and began counting years not with the birth of Jesus Christ but with the founding of the Republic. Year I therefore began in September 1792. The calendar was scientific, patriotic, and antireligious, effacing all holidays and even Sundays. Rosalie warned Jules, "This new calendar created by [Gilbert] Romme...does not realize the abyss beneath its feet."[59] She saw that new policies on religious practice were upsetting people without benefit: "The religious innovations, or rather the attacks on religion, seem to me premature and maddening at this moment when they afflict sensitive and timorous souls....No religious wars! That's the cry of the faithful. Honor divinity and humanity." Creating religious strife was "like adding to our enemies' ranks and cause[d] more bloodshed in the Republic." She therefore advised Jules, when he was in St. Malo in November, "Preach the love of God and of men."[60]

As part of Jules's job was to oversee religious reeducation, Rosalie recommended moderation. She told Jules at the end of February, "It is not with the sword or blade or fire that one destroys prejudice or habits, but with the torch of reason and the soft and triumphant armory of persuasion. I recommend to you the latter."[61] Other times, she generally promoted the same virtues she had always taught her son: kindness, hard work, and self-control. At the beginning of his mission, she advised him, "Do not take the beaten path, but make your own by following the light of justice and the traces of prudence. Be the master of yourself before you lead others."[62] She was particularly worried that he not say anything to make enemies, especially after the Girondins were executed in October. She told him, "You must be an active guard over yourself. You must be a vigilant sentinel whose conscience never sleeps."[63] In many ways, her relationship with Jules during the Terror was a more mature version of their relationship in the Old Regime. She even cited the same author she had loved to read together with him as a child, this time a little distorted to match the ideology of the Terror: "'Kindness goes further than violence,' says our good La Fontaine, and kindness with republican severity is not as incompatible as one would think."[64]

The Revolution became even more of a family affair to Rosalie once her son was in government, because it literally became family business. Recall the way she "adopted" Tarbes as her hometown when Jules was sent there in the spring of 1793. Her biological relationship to her son mingled with the *patrie*'s metaphorical relationship to Jules. He was the son of France as well as Rosalie's child. She understood that her needs and the needs of the Revolution had become intertwined when, in February 1794, she wrote, "My dear son, be virtuous in the name of a mother's love. Work as hard as you are strong, be as zealous as you are capable, and know, without being prideful, that your existence brings prosperity to the Republic and happiness to your tender parents."[65] Just as Rosalie had taught her children how to live virtuously, the Revolution became a mother figure that fostered virtue. After all, "[Virtue] is the mother of liberty, equality, and fraternity. These three daughters cannot live outside its bosom," she wrote that same February.[66] A few days later, she reminded Jules to be virtuous "in the name of a mother's love" as well as for the "prosperity [of] the Republic."[67] Virtue, motherhood, and the Republic became one.

The Revolution was also mother-like in that it helped her son reach new heights in his career. Rosalie had always hoped her children would accomplish great things, but they were held back by the world of privilege. By this point, Rosalie was convinced that the Revolution had saved Jules from a virtuous yet largely inconsequential existence. Now there were no limits on his ability to accumulate authority in the name of virtue and to spread his kindness, fairness, and even "republican severity" throughout France.[68] She was proud that he "will be, for the *patrie*, for your peers, what you are to your father and mother who adore you."[69] The nation would learn what Rosalie had always believed, that her son was an exceptionally talented individual, a born leader. She was delighted when she realized that the Committee of Public Safety saw talent in her son. At the beginning of his mission, she wrote, "The confidence that the Committee of Public Safety accorded you prompts you to lift yourself above yourself, to develop a strong character that justifies the importance of your commissions."[70] Nothing was more influential in her political ideology than her relationship with her son, whose career she nurtured and whose success she credited to a Revolution that was like a second mother to her child. In this way, she adopted the Revolution—and the Terror—as if it were as dear to her as the son who was an instrument of it.[71]

Rosalie embraced the Terror in spite of her earlier opposition to violence. Amazingly, even during Jules's troubles with Carrier, she told him that "this period in your political career will always be precious to my heart."[72] Why?

There seem to be three reasons. First, in spite of his challenges, Jules was successfully forging a career as an influential civil servant. The praise he received from the committee members and others buoyed Rosalie's spirits. When she read about his positive reception in St. Malo, "tears of tenderness and pleasure deliciously wet the eyes of the most sensitive of mothers."[73] Second, this stage in their life gave Rosalie an opportunity to work cooperatively with her maturing son in a new way. He was eighteen years old when he began his missions, and he had enough responsibility and experience to be independent of his parents. Yet he also still relied on his mother's letters for encouragement and consolation. Rosalie was proud of his accomplishments and comforted by his continued need for her care. Third, she was able to make an impact on the Revolution by being her son's counselor. As women's public roles were being reduced, her private relationships became dramatically more political.

Year II was a significant year for the Revolution and for Rosalie; untangling its complexity provides insight into how an obscure woman from the suburbs became an apologist for the Reign of Terror. The origins of the Terror were complex, a combination of political and psychological triggers. But Rosalie offers another, more personal perspective. With her son in a position of power, Rosalie adopted the government's policies because they were part of her son's new identity as a young adult in the New Regime. Rosalie's position within the family was central to her revolutionary experience. Her position as *mère de famille*, and especially as mother of a member of government, was the prism through which she understood the Revolution. Furthermore, this gendered citizenship was not limiting from her point of view. She believed that women's attributes of sensitivity, loyalty, and strength of conviction made them excellent, perhaps the best, republicans.

6

Thermidor

The earth is completely covered in snow, and the poor little birds do not know where to go. It froze last night, and our vines are damaged. Several of our trees lost branches from the weight of the snow. Our sad lambs cannot leave the stable. Everything is in a very bad state. I wish the snow would melt, but that does not look as nice.

JULES JULLIEN, MARCH 31, 1785[1]

The streets, the houses are ornamented with garlands, flowers, and greenery. Everything that I catch sight of from my window is a vision, brilliant and magnificent. Everyone is energized; they come and go with the serenity and gaiety of a festival day. Nature, hearts reunite to render you homage!

ROSALIE JULLIEN, APRIL 9, 1794[2]

JULES WROTE THE first passage above in March 1785. It was a description of Romans that he sent to his father when he was ten years old. The second comes from his mother. This time she wrote to a grown-up Jules in April 1794, from the banks of the Seine rather than the Isère, among fields of billowing tricolor banners rather than quivering walnut trees.

Both of those passages discuss nature, and yet Rosalie's is an aberration. Nearly every other word of her revolutionary correspondence was devoted to politics. Suddenly, this opening paragraph stands out.

The images of beauty, growth, and renewal stand in stark contrast to the other elements of her urban habitat. Just four days earlier, Danton and his allies had fallen under the guillotine, the most recent in a series of political purges. In only a few months, Rosalie's family would be at risk when the Terror collapsed on the reigning Montagnards. The political climate matched Jules's description of hopeless snowbound animals more than Rosalie's description of hopeful blooms. Why did she pause to reflect on garlands in the midst of so much turbulence?

Maybe Rosalie's reverie here was a natural reaction to the situation, a way of living in a terrifying world. She sought something beautiful, natural, and permanent. April's blossoms would continue to bud long after the fires of fury and terror had fizzled and turned to ash. And yet that brief description of nature, emanating from a context of death, reminds us in another way of Jules's letter from the Old Regime. His note depicted a natural landscape that was both awe inspiring and menacing. The ten-year-old Jules made a complex observation about his emotions in that short postscript. The snow was killing the vine, suffocating the lambs, and scattering the birds, which caused him distress. And yet the white veil it formed over the landscape was pretty, and he knew that the subsequent slush, although a hopeful sign of rejuvenation, would be messy and murky. At the last moment, he clung to the snow rather than to change.

Rosalie came to embrace the ideology of the Terror in large part because of her son's position as an elite member of government. But under the veil of seamless snow, the soothing ideology of virtuous terror, Rosalie sometimes witnessed the damage it wrought. An essential part of Rosalie's story lies in the misgivings she felt, the glimpses she had into the death the Terror caused, and the danger it posed to her loved ones. She clung to the veil of silence despite this unease; there were emotional advantages of doing so. But eventually, she would face the inevitable change of political seasons.

Death took many forms during the Revolution. The frequent use of the guillotine during the Terror inaugurated a new phase of revolutionary violence.[3] One historian claims that the technique of beheading actually decreased emotional responses to death. Citing a small number of eyewitnesses, she concludes that the executions were too quick to elicit a reaction from the crowd.[4] Rosalie's example contradicts that thesis. She experienced pity, curiosity, "horror of blood," and fear of humanity's degeneration because of the guillotine. Although Rosalie never mentioned witnessing executions, she went to the Revolutionary Tribunal frequently. At the Tribunal, seeing the condemned, for whom death was so close, was an emotional experience for her. When the twenty-one Girondins were tried in October 1793, she reported on their trial with great interest:

> Vergniaux and Gensonné had the most somber and dark counte-nances. Brissot did not have a moral physiognomy. His face said nothing. Fonfrède and Ducos looked like peasants from Danube, their hair hiding most of their faces, which did not express any-thing remarkable. Sillery Brulard was pale because he has gout. La Source looked like death and coughed as if he had tuberculosis. He had a little rage in his eyes. Valasé…[had] the intention of selling his life dearly.…I saw Madame Roland, who looked well possessed, because of her posture, her tone, her elegance, and her ease. Is that not touching, especially for an accused?[5]

The interest she demonstrated in taking a prolonged and detailed look into the faces of the condemned contradicts the claim that onlookers failed to make connections with the victims.

Later, Rosalie reported the Girondins' deaths to Jules by passing along the report of a friend who was at the execution. Both she and the friend were interested in the emotions and conditions of each indi-vidual. As before, Rosalie exhibited considerable fascination, and also some pity:

> [Our friend] came the day before yesterday to give us an exact account of the execution of the twenty-one [Girondin] crimi-nals, to which he was a witness, [standing] just two feet from the fatal machine. Sillery was the first, and Brissot the sev-enth. Each one brought the nuances of his character, and the

leaders, Brissot, Vergniaud, and Gensonné, did not show fear except for their extreme paleness. The young Fonfrède, Ducos, Mainvieilles, Duprat, and Duchastel wanted to enliven their last moments with patriotic chants, and this changed the nature of things except for the livid expressions on their faces. But let us throw a veil over all of this.[6]

As in many instances, the useful "veil" covered complicated feelings, including remorse. However, Rosalie did admit that the suite of executions caused her to worry over what the killing was doing to human nature. "I like it when they punish the culpable but not when they joke about the sadness [of it]," she told Jules.[7]

Rosalie's faith in justice comforted her when the Girondins were executed, but that faith was sometimes tested. When a good friend was arrested without cause, she and Marc-Antoine spent three months speaking with authorities to try to secure his release. The friend, Saint-Cyr Bodin, was from Lyon, a city where resistance to Paris's authority maintained a stronghold. His Lyonnais background was the reason for his arrest, as Rosalie pointed out to her son: "Saint-Cyr Bodin is in la Force [Prison], arrested like a Lyonnais....the troubles in Lyon make it a crime to be Lyonnais."[8] Rosalie and Marc-Antoine had "much work to do and much chagrin." They did "much to get him acquitted" and were finally successful at the end of November.[9] Bodin was not the only friend the Julliens fought for; two others were arrested that fall as well.

After her friends were arrested, Rosalie made an observation. She wrote, "In moments of crisis, every man is like Caesar's wife. It is not enough to be innocent; you have to avoid being suspected."[10] This realization is significant because it lends support to a thesis advanced by William Reddy. Reddy sees the Terror as a period of severe emotional discipline. Jacobin ideology borrowed from Rousseau's *Social Contract*, which stated that sovereignty resided in the general will of the people. The general will was not necessarily the majority opinion, because individuals could have a false sense of what they really wanted. The general will was the true will of the people, and it was possible for only a few enlightened people to express it. They would then force the others to be free, to join the general will. The Jacobins believed they possessed the general will. Those who resisted joining the general will became counterrevolutionary, outside the nation, and subject to persecution. Reddy adds that a critical way to adhere to the general will was to comply with the emotional expectations the Jacobins set. Citizens had to feel patriotism in their hearts. This positive feeling for the *patrie* was thought to be natural; counterrevolutionaries were either devious or misled and too dangerous to spare.[11]

According to Reddy's thesis, citizens were compelled to feel patriotic, secure, and innocent because feelings of fear were supposed to indicate culpability. The Terror therefore led to an environment of "emotional suffering" because fear of the guillotine was present in the guilty and the innocent alike, but expressing this feeling could endanger one's life. To avoid accusation, citizens had to express feelings of innocence and security, not dread.[12] The command to feel patriotic was in truth very limiting, especially in a period when danger lurked in the form of civil war, foreign war on several fronts, and Revolutionary Tribunals that sent accused counterrevolutionaries to the Place de la Révolution for execution.

Rosalie usually expressed support of Jacobin ideology and its emotional requirements. In the same letter where she complained about her friends being wrongly arrested, she wrote, "These arrests burden and concern everyone. However, they are so necessary to the public good [*chose publique*] that even the victims cannot complain if they are truly republicans."[13] This comment came weeks after the beginning of the Terror. She similarly reassured Jules in December, "But, my friend, laws are only made for troublemakers.... good men, by carrying justice in their hearts," had nothing to worry about.[14]

In rare moments, however, Rosalie also admitted that this idealism was difficult to maintain. In fact, after explaining that certain activities, like popular festivals, filled citizens with positive feelings, she also wrote, "Terror as the order of the day [has been] as disastrous for our friends as for our enemies." Perhaps she was thinking about her friends like Bodin, in prison. She concluded, "It would take a book to explain that this paralysis was an epidemic that only spared the most robust republicans." Only the most "robust" were not "paralyzed" by the emotional requirements established under the Terror. Although she confessed her "ardent love and concern...for the Republic," she also admitted that "the experience of four years of Revolution" felt "more like four centuries."[15] Casting a veil over the fear and violence was simpler than revealing the sham behind the curtain, but it was exhausting.

Rosalie's gender influenced her desire to conceal her negative feelings. The emotional language that Reddy cites came mostly from men. After all, they were the active citizens seeking public office and leading the Revolution; they had a clear political purpose for expressing their feelings publicly. Women seem to have had less at stake when submitting to an emotional regime; they were cordoned off from public life in many significant ways. However, the burden of the emotional regime was different. The fear of the guillotine might have affected men and women equally, and the feelings of patriotism might have been equally expected of both sexes, but while men could prove their revolutionary zeal through speeches, activity in the Convention, or on the battlefield, women had limited opportunities to prove themselves—especially during the Terror, when women's assembly was banned. Women's feelings were therefore even more important for their safety; they had few other methods for proving their patriotism.

Reddy argues that the nineteenth century witnessed a new attitude toward politics and emotions that was a direct result of the experience of the Terror. The shift occurred just before Robespierre's fall. The new opinion asserted that public life was to be the realm of reason, while private life was a place for emotional freedom.[16] In public, once again, "[s]uperficial submission was quite sufficient," as it had been when subjects bowed to the king.[17] A full range of emotions was permitted in the private sphere, where emotions were understood to be "emanations of a truer self."[18] This was the response to a regime that had relied so much on feeling that it had ultimately stifled the freedom to feel naturally.[19]

Rosalie made this turn toward privacy even earlier than Reddy notes. In May 1794, at the beginning of the hundred days that saw the greatest number of guillotine victims, she wrote to Jules about a place of refuge deep within her inner thoughts. "It is in small things that man is great. It is in the obscurity of the interior of his heart where he develops his goodness," she told him.[20] The timing is significant. Jules had returned to Bordeaux for a second time, following his first trip earlier that spring. In Bordeaux, he developed a reputation for growing extremism. Although he had condemned Carrier's actions in Nantes, in Bordeaux he fought against what he termed "moderatism." He oversaw the executions of Girondins and drove others, including Pétion, to commit suicide. He made significant political enemies in the process. Other government officials, Tallien and Ysabeau, resented the young Jules's authority and refused to take his orders.

Rosalie said little about Jules's activities in Bordeaux except to remind him of "small things." In addition to the widespread emotional suffering that likely affected many during the Terror, Rosalie felt the added strain, and possibly the guilt, of being the mother of a young and rather impetuous representative of the Committee of Public Safety. Her retreat to privacy was part of an impulse to remind her son about their family life and the values they had cultivated in Romans. While in Bordeaux, Jules received another letter that emphasized private spaces: "I admire the war heroes," his mother wrote. "I respect the republican heroes in the tribune, on the battlefield, and in all public functions. But I adore the heroes in their bathrobes, whose sweet morals and lovable wisdom make humanity smile with gladness."[21] This praise for private morality was not a direct contradiction of her assertion that Jules's public career was dear to her. But it does mark a turning point, most pronounced in the late spring of 1794, when Rosalie realized that the Terror was larger than all of them.

It is not surprising that Rosalie sought relief, emotional refuge, from time to time. In this context we can better understand her brief homage to nature quoted in the epigraph. It is interesting that Rosalie wrote such a dedication to nature at that time. For much of her life, she had resisted Marc-Antoine's and Jules's insistence on nature's superiority to society, even though she valued nature in small doses. She was not as impressed by Rousseau's apologies to nature as the men in her family were. "No, we are not made to live in the woods and walk on all fours like one wants to when one reads your great friend J. J. Rousseau," she told Jules in June 1792, paraphrasing Rousseau's nemesis, Voltaire.[22] How surprising it is, then, that she wrote just six months later, "I would rather live in the forest than with men [because] the Revolution has evoked such passion that one hardly recognizes man."[23] A year after that, the Terror was in full swing, and she further blurred the line between civilization and the savage natural world. When the Girondins were executed, she wrote, "We must not, in the face of so many victims, who were justly snuffed out by the blade of the law, extinguish our humanity and the sense of pity that distinguishes man from the rest of the animals."[24] As violence increased among people, nature's call grew louder. In the wilderness that had previously not seemed as appealing as genteel city life, Rosalie now saw comfort and safety in nature, whose beasts were not as savage as men. If nature was another emotional refuge, added to the "interior of [her] heart," then we can better understand the pause she took in the opening of her letter from April 1794. Her effort to overcome politics and focus on more permanent things was a manifestation of the "veil" she threw over events that disturbed her.

Then, on 9 Thermidor (or July 27, 1794) Jules's nemesis, Tallien, led the charge against Robespierre and the others, shouting, "Down with the tyrant!" And in a moment, the Revolution pivoted again, and the sun set on the Mountain. Robespierre, Couthon, and many others were killed the following day.

Jules was in Bordeaux and knew nothing about the sudden turn of events. Rosalie had to explain: "[T]he infamous Robespierre [wounded] the Republic, leading excellent patriots to their fall. I feel hopeless....Paris and the Republic were two fingers from their fall. The genius of France awoke, and if ever the people of Paris agreed, it was in this famous night where destiny presented them with the choice between a man and the authority he constituted." This reading of the Thermidorian Reaction is so measured that we can almost see her steeling herself in preparation for the unknown. Her friends were dead, and her son was closely associated with them. She assured Jules that his father "is carrying himself like a wise and true republican, but that is his usual way. He is the enemy of intrigue and above all of this baseness. He witnessed this storm with the calm and wisdom and pain of a good man seeing a crime relived so many times in the annals of virtue."[25] Whether genuine or not, her expression of relief over Robespierre's fall was a smart political maneuver.

In reality, this White Terror was surely the most frightening time for Rosalie and her family, who feared that Jules would be among its victims. She likely felt genuine anger toward Robespierre because of the position her family was in as a result of their relationship with him. She had regretted the violence of the Terror, which he had helped propel. And yet Rosalie had enjoyed dinner conversations with "the Incorruptible" while he tried to hold the nation together in Year II, met with him as he helped promote her son's career, and cared for him when he was sick. Although the entire Jullien family renounced Robespierre and regretted his excesses, their loss was surely complicated. Because of the very high stakes of Rosalie's letters, her true feelings, however complex and contradictory they might have been, are truly difficult to know. To express any sadness over Robespierre's demise would be dangerous.

For his part, Jules was rather easily convinced that Robespierre had in fact become an outlaw. But that did not protect him from closely following his former friend's path. Jules's conflicts in the provinces haunted him for years. Ysabeau and Tallien from Bordeaux and Carrier from Nantes accused Jules of being Robespierre's crony, at which point he was sent to Plessis Prison, where he was detained for fourteen months, throughout the Thermidorian Convention.[26] While Jules was imprisoned, Rosalie wrote him only short notes and sent along small provisions to comfort him. Cloth, an ivory knife, and some silver were in the first package.[27] Her main efforts during those months of Jules's detainment were directed toward securing his release.

To help her son, she did what she had always done: she wrote many letters in search of support and testimonials of Jules's patriotism. As the Republican Mother, Rosalie defined the quality of her family's values. Her evidence in support of Jules's innocence was that "nothing other than the public good was ever felt within his soul" because he had "his mother's sensibility." In fact, she never mentioned his name but wrote, a dozen or more times in each letter, "my son...my son."[28] She also used emotions as proof, writing to one man, "[My son] arrived with the tranquility and firmness of innocence."[29] Rosalie had a difficult task: defending her son and his patriotism in Year II while simultaneously denouncing Robespierre and his policies. To the recipient of one of her letters, she claimed that Robespierre "duped" good Republicans, and she called the Terror a "monster" that "held even the National Convention under a harness of fire."[30] She expressed relief that the Terror was over, telling one woman, "My husband and I, secretly at home, we deplored the rigor [of the Terror]." In an effort to explain the contradiction between that statement and the fact that her family helped enforce that rigor, she added, "For us, as for all of France, a domineering yoke...reduced us to silence while driving us toward an abyss of evil."[31]

This woman to whom Rosalie wrote in August 1795 was none other than Tallien's wife. Thérésa Tallien was a couple of years older than Jules. She was the daughter of a financier and married an aristocrat in 1788. Her love affair with Tallien began after her husband emigrated from France. She divorced him, and then she was arrested as the wife of an émigré in Bordeaux. Tallien released her, became her partner, and finally married her in December 1794. Love affairs did not end there for this colorful person, who had a daughter by Tallien named Thermidor. In short, Thérésa and Rosalie were dissimilar in many ways. But they were critically connected in the summer of 1795, and Rosalie swallowed her pride as she addressed Thérésa: "You are a mother, and I am a mother. This similarity must unite our hearts. You are a woman, and I am a woman. The natural sensitivity of our sex must bring us together even more.... *Citoyenne*, I write honestly and with the frankness inspired by two feelings: love for justice and the love of a mother."[32] She then asked her and her husband to rescind their charges against Jules.

Rosalie's letter to Thérésa was different from the others she wrote when soliciting support. Thérésa was the only woman to whom Rosalie wrote. She was also the only person who was not already a friend or acquaintance. And Rosalie wrote to her from a position that was unlike any of her other postures: as a mother writing to a mother. Rosalie relied on this similarity between them to give her action legitimacy, to supersede any other dissimilarity the two might have had, and to overcome the distance between strangers.

The rest of her letter listed many of the same points as her other letters seeking help for her son. She explained that he was the victim of "the cruelest injustice." She also included her formulaic denunciation of the Terror, writing that her family "was far from supportive of even the least of the injustices committed under the reign of Terror." But she also included some other thoughts in this letter to Thérésa that reflect the different audience. She exclaimed that her son's imprisonment "strikes mortal blows in the breast of a virtuous family." To prove that virtue, she explained, "My husband, the most virtuous and gentlest of men, who, in the terrible chaos of a revolution, forced even his enemies to respect him, consecrated seventeen years of his life to the education of his son. He preached examples of all of the virtues, which he engraved on [his son's] heart.... [I swear that] never in my son's childhood was he corrupted with a single fault, and that his filial piety is without stain."[33] Finally, she closed by signing that she was, "with fraternal feelings, the mother of Jullien."[34] From that relationship, she derived the authority to testify to her son's lifelong morality. She hoped another mother would understand.

Jules was released from prison fourteen months after he arrived. During a routine check on the status of her son's case, Rosalie was told anticlimactically that he was now free to go. Whether her efforts on her son's behalf helped save his life is not certain, but they provide us a vantage point from which to view the lives of two women whose fates crossed during a turbulent moment in French history.

The months of waiting added to the stresses of losing many Jacobin friends to the guillotine and concluded the final chapter in Rosalie's revolutionary experience. Her misgivings about the Terror mingled with her pride in Jules's accomplishments and her affection for the Montagnards. All feelings, positive and negative, were present in Year II. After Thermidor, the variety of powerful emotions diminished until she was left with just one: determination to save Jules. In the process, she lost faith in the power of the French people to live up to the ideals of 1789. In fact, while in the first five years of the Revolution she had maintained hope that her country was on an inevitable course of success, by 1802 she could not discern what the future looked like. Furthermore, the bloodshed that had been committed in the name of the Revolution, which she had regretted anyway, she now saw as completely unjustified. The sense of progress toward a greater good had left her, to be replaced by uncertainty, frailty, and danger.

Rosalie never again discussed current events in her letters. During the Terror, she had begun to seek emotional refuges, tending increasingly toward privacy and the safety of her home and family life. After Jules's release from prison, she excluded politics completely from her letter writing, even though she wrote longer letters in the early nineteenth century than ever before. The dashed hopes that the New Regime would breed virtue, the weight of the veil that concealed her fears, the trauma of Jules's imprisonment—all culminated in a definitive break with the Revolution in 1795. She never looked back.

It was clear she had closed the revolutionary chapter of her life when she wrote to Jules in 1802, "The book of the future is closed to everyone, so let's look to the present and not poison it with the uncertainty of the future. One has to live like a mole in its hole and try to be happy."[35] She lived in a new, post-Thermidorian world and advised her son to think always about "the actual circumstances, completely forgetting the past, because times have changed. And like a chameleon, one must do no less than change pretense, course, and perspective."[36] Her change of course entailed concentrating on new priorities. In the nineteenth century, Rosalie began a new chapter.

7

Generations

IN 1798, JULES disappointed Rosalie, perhaps for the first time in his life. Jules fathered a child. At least, he and the mother believed that he was the father; Rosalie had her doubts. Jules met the mother in Italy. Rosalie never referred to her by name, but instead called her a "Siren," a "vile object that was momentarily the object of your affections."[1] Jules did not appreciate his mother's critical words, but she continued anyway, accusing the woman of doing everything she could to humiliate him through her indiscretion and immodesty. She said that Jules was equally prideful, too proud to admit that he was manipulated and too stubborn to listen to his parents and walk away from the affair. Eventually, Jules listened to his mother and lived separately from the woman and the child, whose birth certificate reads Emile-Gracchioli Jullien, born May 3, 1798. The name Emile is of course homage to Rousseau. Gracchioli sounds like Gracchus Babeuf, the radical Jules befriended in prison in 1794.[2] Jules honored two friends when he named the child he clearly believed was his offspring. But Rosalie told him that this was "no mistake in the manner of Jean-Jacques Rousseau," referencing the many children Rousseau fathered and sent to the foundling home.[3]

Emile died a year later, on June 11, 1799.[4] Rosalie said nothing about it. Jules was just being freed from prison in Naples. (Once again he had been associated with an authority figure who fell out of favor in France.)[5] His release, and his mother's relief, coincided almost exactly with his son's death.

This episode in Jules's life was never directly mentioned again. Only once did Rosalie write vaguely about not wanting to repeat a "bad experience."[6] In an eerie way, this sequence of events was similar to a time in Marc-Antoine's life that was also never written about. Marc-Antoine's first marriage, of which Mably had disapproved, was over quickly, along with the life of his first child. Just as Marc-Antoine married a second time, Jules also enjoyed a long marriage following the dissolution of his first family. In both generations, the first family seems to have been forgotten by everyone. Perhaps this similarity occurred to Rosalie and was a small factor in why she loved Jules's second partner so much. They shared a role in common in relation to these two Jullien men.

In this phase of Rosalie's life, the Revolution was a memory. Like a bad love affair, it rarely made an appearance in her conversations once it was done. Her new topics were entirely domestic. Health, family finances, marriage, and children occupied her letters, which were even longer than her revolutionary correspondence. As she seems to have come full circle in her occupations and values at the end of her life, the question lingers: What lasting impact, if any, did the Revolution have on her?

Rosalie searched for a wife for Jules throughout 1800, at his urgent request. "We will find you a perfect wife on the condition that you become a perfect man," she teased in August.[7] At that point, Jules was in Switzerland, traveling with the Army of Italy and writing a republican newspaper. His job in the army carried him far and wide. Meanwhile, in Paris, Rosalie found her ideal daughter. Rosalie and Marc-Antoine went to see an acquaintance in Charenton in the fall. Pierre-Claude Nioche had, like Marc-Antoine, been a regicide seven years earlier. He and his wife had just lost their older daughter from illness. "With what sensitivity we will share his pain, and with what interest will I examine his younger daughter!" Rosalie explained. "I am still searching for a Sophie for my Emile." Indeed, her "Emile" (had the memory of the other Emile already faded?) would become the husband of a bona fide Sophie: Marthe Jouvence Sophie Nioche.[8] Of course, everyone called her by her third name.

It is striking that death seems once again to have brought about a marriage for a Jullien man. Marc-Antoine's first wife had been gone only a few months before he and Rosalie began their life together. A second death in Sophie's family, that of her female cousin, caused her great "despair over this double loss" in February 1801. While Sophie's mother left home to join her mourning relatives, Rosalie brought Sophie to live with her. Jules, on leave in Paris and courting Sophie, moved into his uncle Bernard's home to maintain propriety. And then, at what must have been a difficult time for young Sophie, Jules proposed marriage. Rosalie explained to Virginie, "Yesterday her mother arrived. I put Sophie back into her arms.... We delicately let Sophie tell her mother that [Jules] had made the overture of marriage, and we are waiting for the results." Rosalie feared that because Sophie was so young, her parents might not approve. Meanwhile, Jules prepared for good news by planning to relocate back to France. "If the [marriage proposal] is successful, he will ask Bonaparte, of whom he has never asked anything, for a position in Paris or in the interior, which he thinks he will get," Rosalie told Virginie.[9]

Sophie and Jules were married in 1801. She was only sixteen years old; Jules was nine years her senior. Rosalie loved her daughter-in-law. She was contemplative, quiet, and serious. She was not a passionate girl, but she was tranquil and sensible, more mature in demeanor than in age. She was, most important, "pure as heaven."[10] Rosalie later told Jules, "I love your wife: she is good, sweet, she has more reason and judgment than normal for her age." She praised Sophie's "simple taste," her "natural tendency for privacy and quiet," which were "two safeguards of virtue." She was also "beautiful without thinking so."[11]

Still employed in the army, Jules left his bride in Paris while he lived in Holland in the summer of 1801. Marc-Antoine had moved back to Romans for a while; Auguste had also attached himself to the army after a year of struggling to find an appointment. Alone together, Rosalie and Sophie developed a friendship. Rosalie wrote to Marc-Antoine, "I am infinitely happy with [Jules's] wife. We spend the mornings together. Your room is our study, a happy place."[12] Rosalie connected with her daughter-in-law over their mutual fondness for reading. In addition to studying together in the mornings, Sophie read aloud to Rosalie for

two hours every evening.[13] Rosalie wanted to develop a strong relationship with her new daughter. "I hope that my son's wife will be his
mother's friend. I am trying to make that so, with success," she reported
to Jules.[14]

She also hoped that Jules and Sophie would enjoy the companionship of a modern marriage. In February 1802, she counseled, "Be
happy, my children. Through your confidence and your mutual tenderness think, both of you, how the most solid happiness is in the
union of two souls who listen to each other and love each other."[15]
Rosalie wrote that advice during an especially meaningful period in
her marriage. Her health and that of Marc-Antoine were in serious
decline. Rosalie relied on Marc-Antoine's support during slow prom-
enades. In December 1800, she told Jules, who was at that moment
in Feldkirch, Switzerland, "We go frequently to the Tuileries and the
Luxembourg [Gardens]. This winter I adopted a system of walking
that I think suits my health … I would not have the courage to practice without the arms of my Hercules, your dear father."[16] Although
she had felt the symptoms of rheumatism for twenty years, by 1802,
she had periods where her movement was severely restricted. She
called herself "a woman of glass, whom the slightest movement could
break, forced to live in bed or a chair."[17] Her doctor recommended
fresh air and adding grapes to her diet to increase her bowel move-
ments and, presumably, improve her joint pain. Rosalie thought that
made a lot of sense and recommended it to her children again and
again.

As her body grew stiffer, she continued to be grateful for her husband's care. She explained to Jules and Sophie in 1803, "Picture me: I
have painful convulsions at night that occasion vomiting. I only sleep
with the help of opium. I do not leave my room, where your papa treats
me with care that appears always renewed to me, not bored as a man
with a wife who is always wailing and suffering must be." She therefore
recommended to the young couple, "That [affection] is where you collect the prize of a solid friendship and a perfect union. Lay the foundation of [your marriage] in your youth because there will come a time

when, perhaps, it will be put to the test. That is when we must be happy to love each other, help each other, carry life's burdens."[18]

Sleep was problematic for both Rosalie and Marc-Antoine. To sleep through her aches, Rosalie took opium most nights.[19] The difference between her sleep habits and those of her teenage daughter-in-law struck Rosalie once when she was writing to Marc-Antoine: "How wonderful to be seventeen years old! My daughter sleeps through the morning without any cares....Everything is grand in the best of all possible worlds with the magic lenses of a seventeen-year-old."[20] Marc-Antoine's insomnia worsened over the course of the first decade of the nineteenth century. In 1807, he barely slept for most of the year.[21] Lemonade, footbaths, and almond milk failed to help, so Rosalie and Marc-Antoine took a trip to the country to let nature cure him. The vacation had mixed results for him, but Rosalie was able to enjoy long walks.[22] Between the two sexagenarians, Marc-Antoine's health appears to have declined more severely than Rosalie's. In 1803, tremors began. "He is becoming a trembler, or, simply, he trembles, which makes the use of the plume difficult," Rosalie told Jules in July.[23] A poignant post-script added by a very shaky hand finished after a few sentences with, "That is enough for my poor trembling fingers."[24] These tremors, which they diagnosed as sciatica, in addition to his frequent headaches, caused Marc-Antoine to become "profoundly sad."[25]

Rosalie usually maintained a less serious outlook. Despite her troubles, she faced her winter years with good humor, telling her sister-in-law, "Death and I, we smile at each other from a distance," adding that it takes a Herculean blow to kill a woman after she passes a certain age.[26] Laughing at herself, she reported, "My figure bears the impression of my aches. I am old and wrinkled like an eighty-year-old."[27] But if she joked about her body, she was disquieted by the state of her mind. "I am losing my memory; I am becoming a fool," she confided to Virginie.[28] At first she blamed her age, writing in 1807, "I often repeat myself. *My age is the cause of it*. I am old to the point of babbling."[29] But a couple of years later, she wondered if "this mischievous opium, which I have used so much," was the problem.[30]

Rosalie believed that the root of all of her health problems was her first pregnancy.[31] For that reason, she worried constantly over Sophie's health throughout her daughter-in-law's childbearing years. Soon after Jules and Sophie married, Sophie became pregnant, and she stayed nearly constantly pregnant thereafter, until she had produced seven children. The first, Auguste, was born in the spring of 1802. After Adolphe (1803), Saint-Cyr (1804), and Alfred (1805) were born, Stéphanie, the longed-for daughter, arrived in the spring of 1807.[32] Alphonse and Félix joined the family later. Saint-Cyr, named for Jules's closest friend, was the only child not to live into adulthood.

Beginning in 1801, then, there never ceased to be cause for conversation over pregnancy, birth, and child care.[33] These topics afforded Rosalie a welcome distraction from her own problems. She showered Sophie with advice about how to alleviate the physical tolls of pregnancy. As always, diet was emphasized: milk and bouillon. To supplement her personal experiences, she asked her doctor to make suggestions. "Doctor Fanchette approves of your bouillons.... If you want the recipe for mine, here it is: thirty black prunes, well boiled, melted with an ounce of marrow. If someone else tells you a different [recipe] you like more, it's your choice."[34] She also begged Sophie to stay away from strenuous exercise and heavy lifting, nervous about her young age and small frame.[35] "My good friend, take care of yourself and be aware that the first delivery affects your health for the rest of your life. I say this in principle because, sadly, I am an example [of poor health resulting from pregnancy]. It is from carrying too heavy a burden after delivering my son, your husband, that I am sick today. At least mothers' experiences help the daughters."[36] Near the end of Sophie's pregnancy, Rosalie recommended having a doctor bleed her, probably believing it would help reduce swelling.[37]

After the first child was born, Rosalie advised a long break, telling Jules that "this dear girl ... already gave us such charming proof of your conjugal love."[38] When Sophie was soon pregnant again, Rosalie's first reaction was to scold Jules for not leaving his young wife alone. She urged him to follow her advice better after the second birth. She wrote, "My lovely friend, since you will have a beautiful nursing wife, I hope you will respect her duties and her interests. She needs at least two years of rest. Poor little thing. At age nineteen to be a mother twice in only twenty-one months. It proves courage and tenderness, and that merits your generosity and a little sacrifice."[39] By the fourth pregnancy, Rosalie wrote, "I would hit you if I were near you." She called him treacherous for putting Sophie in the position of fulfilling "the task that she has already more than fulfilled. One lets a good earth repose. One leaves a poor woman alone sometimes."[40] Indeed, Rosalie was very concerned about the toll these many children were taking on Sophie. "It could kill a poor petite woman," she warned.[41]

Regardless of Rosalie's disapproval, Jules and Sophie reproduced several more times. Rosalie was present at two of her grandchildren's births. In July 1805, Sophie had her fourth son, Alfred, while living in Amiens. Rosalie had thought she would arrive at their house with many days to spare before Sophie began to labor, but this was not the case. She arrived at three in the afternoon on a Sunday, Sophie went to bed feeling sick at seven, "and before ten o'clock we have the *poupon* [baby doll]." They were "quite upset that the boy was not a girl, but very happy that the event went well." As always, Rosalie had hoped for a granddaughter, but when Alfred was born, she was happy that he was "well and very handsome, like the others." She was also comforted by the idea that "the three brothers will help each other in the torturous path of life."[42] This fourth child was only the third living brother because the third child, Saint-Cyr, lived only briefly in 1804. Rosalie probably made the journey to Amiens so that she could help Sophie rest and prevent the premature delivery that had precipitated Saint-Cyr's short life.

Almost exactly three years later, Rosalie again helped her daughter-in-law bring another baby into the world. This time they were all living in Paris. This time was also very special because at last, after four boys, Rosalie was the first to handle the first and only girl. Virginie received this description: "We ate at ten o'clock together. She thought that she still had another month in her term, and after two hours of good sleep, pains woke her. They spread the alarm through the house. Nothing was prepared; there was no help fast enough to assist this little one coming into the world. And, by the grace of the calm courage of my daughter and the maternal love of the grandmother, together we did the chore. I received in my hands, trembling with tenderness and fear, the innocent creature. And the husband, who held his wife from one side, and the domestic servant who held the other, while I was on my knees at the foot of the bed, they all learned from me that Heaven gave them a daughter."[43] Uncle Auguste was to become her godfather, and Virginie the godmother.

Rosalie's concerns for Sophie did not end with pregnancy and labor. In October 1808, she wrote to Sophie about the chest and back pain the young woman had been experiencing. "My dear Jouvence, my tender daughter, my best friend, your illness is caused by the twitching of the nerves around the heart, stomach, and chest.... You are too devoted to your children, and they are hurting you with their demands. You entered young into a punishing career. You have had five children, you nursed four, and once you stop nursing you do not become healthier because you continue the care that is just as tiring." She offered the only advice she knew: "Rest, an eternal rest for this charming stem that yielded such beautiful branches. There are enough [branches]! Now you are a virgin for life.... Get your health back, your happiness, and above all, be assured that your pain is nothing as long as you combat it with reason and care for yourself with the attention that you deserve. You do not love yourself enough."[44] In fact, Sophie did die young, in 1832.

Rosalie's greatest concern for Sophie, however, came in the summer of 1804, when Sophie faced a significant tragedy. Rosalie was surprised to receive a letter on June 8 that announced baby Saint-Cyr's arrival.[45] Like the others, he was born early, but this time there were other problems. He was very small. Rosalie tried to reassure Sophie: "You make children in excerpts because this one only weighs four and a half pounds. But you will add to it with your milk and your care. That has more value than pounds."[46]

But only a few days later, Saint-Cyr perished. When news came of his death, Rosalie and Marc-Antoine empathized with the devastated parents, remembering the death of their second child, Bernard, at sixteen months. Marc-Antoine, who rarely wrote letters even before his hand began to shake, wrote to them at length about the lasting sadness Bernard's death caused him. "Permit me, my dear children, to mix a tear for [Bernard] with those that I shed for you, your loss, and your pain. Time will help heal it without erasing it, as it did for us."[47] Rosalie also recalled being "struck" by the same blow "twenty-four years ago." She wrote, "With bitterness, I toss another tear and a flower on the coffin of my gentle Bernard." She advised Jules and Sophie to support each other in their grief. Rosalie worried considerably about Sophie. She suggested "the distraction of a trip," perhaps to visit her or Sophie's mother. "Give her Nini [Auguste] and Adolphe," her "real comforters," she told Jules.[48] The entire family was distraught. "Tears poured from your brother," she wrote to Jules. "I cannot tell you how much we feel your paternal affliction, how much we worry for your dear wife."[49]

As the family remembered Bernard and Saint-Cyr, did Marc-Antoine's first daughter or Jules's first son come to mind? If Marc-Antoine thought of his other child, he did not write about her.

The pains of pregnancy, the dangers of labor, and the riskiness of premature birth were all significant preoccupations for Sophie and her family for many years. But concern over those topics paled in comparison to another. With each baby, there was a tremendous amount of discussion surrounding Sophie's ability to breast-feed. After the arrival of the first child, many of Rosalie's letters addressed the problem. When Sophie's milk did not come in after Auguste's birth, Rosalie commiserated with the chest pain Sophie felt as a result and called the milk "such a cruel enemy of women when it is turned from its natural destination." "This is not a small affair, being a nurse," she warned Jules and Sophie, noting that it required "heroic courage." It was a battle that this Rousseauist family ardently wished Sophie would win. Jules wrote many nervous letters to his mother, complaining, fretting, and asking for advice. Rosalie prescribed keeping clothing loose over the breasts and keeping "the loins and chest warm to facilitate the running of the milk."[50]

When it was finally determined that Sophie would not nurse little Auguste, it was clear that Jules, Sophie, and Rosalie were disappointed. But Rosalie offered comforting thoughts to both of them. She assured Sophie that failing to nurse the baby herself did not reflect poorly on her maternal dedication, nor did it establish a pattern for the future. She offered four examples of friends, including her sister-in-law and Madame Nugues, who all nursed their second children after not being able to feed their first. She comforted Sophie with the thought that her "maternal bosom" would still be important to her baby, even if it was "not possible to raise him with the maternal breast." To Jules, who was heartbroken over his wife's inability to nurse, and who probably added considerably to Sophie's sense of guilt, she defended Sophie: "She did the most difficult thing. She made you a father."[51]

It then became urgent to procure the services of a wet nurse. While Jules lacked confidence in nurses, Rosalie gave him advice about what to search for and told him not to be too picky. "Do not expect the nurse to be like you, and do not be exacting. A full nipple and cleanliness, that is all you need. People who are less educated are often the most able. Nature, which guides them, is often more valuable than science." She assured her Rousseauist son, who was raised on the idea that wet-nursing corrupted men, that his child would receive benefits from a nurse who was humbler and closer to nature. In that way, she replaced one of Rousseau's values with another. She also warned him not to be cheap: "While I am always in favor of economizing, I do not withhold anything when it comes to life and health. One can repair the loss of money, but the health of a wife, the life of a son, you cannot buy them, and you must sell them at a high price."[52]

Jules found a young woman who was willing to live in their apartment in Amiens with them. Thérèse had just had a child out of wedlock.[53] Because of that moral failing, Jules was worried about the quality of her milk. Rosalie tried to soothe his fears. "I would not hesitate to hire the girl you tell me about if her seduction was only the result of an unhappy weakness and not the effect of libertinage. Her dedication to nursing her child is evidence in her favor.... It is important to learn if her seducer was clean and if she is also. It seems to me that peasant naïveté could easily expose the truth, and that in talking with this poor girl, you could learn all the secrets of her heart. And if she lost her innocence while conserving her *honnêteté*, I advise you not to pass her up." Furthermore, she warned, "If you do not seize this opportunity, I do not see another way than putting your child in the country like the others. Few women would leave their homes without making a small fortune at the expense of yours." She also assured Jules and Sophie that there would not be any emotional damage as a result of wet-nursing. Her reasoning is striking: "I am very happy that [Auguste] is not a girl. Charlotte, whom Madame Nugues could not nurse because of a similar problem, still thinks that her mother does not love her as much as the others whom she did nurse. Mister Auguste, because of his masculinity and his right as the firstborn, has nothing to fear. He will always have a good portion of paternal and maternal tenderness."[54] In fact, Sophie was able to nurse most of her other children, including her daughter, Stéphanie.[55]

It seems that Rosalie succeeded in her desire to be a friend and a supportive second mother to her daughter-in-law. Sophie wrote to Rosalie fondly during her family's travels, despite the frequent interruptions of crying, teething babies and angry toddlers, of which she complained, with good humor, in every letter. Rosalie offered advice when asked but mostly expressed support. However, when it came to the question of vaccinating the children against smallpox, Rosalie was determined that Sophie and Jules must follow her counsel.

The vaccine had arrived in Paris at the beginning of the nineteenth century. Its popularity across Europe reflected a strong desire to try anything that might defend people against the terrible disease. The government established the Vaccine Committee to support trials, encourage local prefects to promote the vaccine, and collect data about its implementation. Historian Yves-Marie Bercé calls this a utopian moment, around 1802, when the political leaders propagated something that was truly "useful" to the welfare of the people.[56] The government called especially upon the midwives and others who consulted with mothers to advertise the benefits of the vaccine. An 1803 law on medicine required every department to have an *école d'accouchement*, or school for childbirth, where the students received lessons on vaccination.[57]

Although smallpox vaccination was largely successful, receiving a vaccine in the early nineteenth century included some risk, and departments reported varying percentages of mortalities following vaccination each year. Madame Dejean's granddaughter nearly died after her injection the same month that Rosalie urged Jules to have Auguste vaccinated.[58] Her friend's scare had little effect on Rosalie as she doggedly pushed Jules and Sophie to vaccinate their son. "I am dying of impatience to know if you had our Auguste vaccinated because smallpox is in Amiens. Have courage and be prompt," she urged.[59] Although she briefly conceded, "I am very relieved that you did not vaccinate him because of the heat," she soon took up her cause again.[60] "I am really upset that you are waiting so long....I am dying to learn if he was vaccinated."[61] When Sophie had him vaccinated, Rosalie wrote, "You did well."[62]

Some historians argue that the generalized acceptance of the vaccine is a sign of the population's faith in new medical practices.[63] Others argue that patriotism led people to follow the government's advice.[64] Perhaps Rosalie's long-standing interest in science and her erstwhile republican dedication played small roles in her enthusiasm for the vaccine, but her primary motivation was certainly her experience with smallpox as a young mother. All three of Rosalie's children contracted the disease. Jules and Auguste recovered from it in 1780 and 1783, respectively. But smallpox bested Bernard when he was barely more than a year old. In 1780, Marc-Antoine wrote to Claude Nugues about his concerns for Jules when, after two days of fever, the pox began to appear. Marc-Antoine started to "cry with the most fearful hopelessness."[65] Three years later, Rosalie wrote to Charlotte Nugues about Auguste: "If you only knew how I have suffered for the past forty-eight hours while my son was thrust into the shadows of death." His fever caused him convulsions that rendered him "hideous."[66] Surely their worries were amplified because by the time Jules and Auguste caught the disease, Bernard had already died of it. Personal experience drove Rosalie to champion the vaccine so that Sophie might be spared the anxiety she endured three times over.

There was another topic on which Rosalie expressed strong feelings. As Jules's family grew almost every year, Rosalie began to discuss budgeting with greater frequency. With few exceptions, all of her nineteenth-century letters discussed good government over the family purse.[67] A significant factor in this preoccupation was the fact that she disagreed with Jules's financial decisions. She balked at his employing three domestic servants, who were "three at the table, which is the costliest thing."[68] He was too cavalier with spending, and his young wife was not old enough to bear the burden of reining in his extravagance, she complained. The topics of health and finances were often closely mingled, and at their core, they both came down to a value that was important to Rosalie now as never before: self-control.

In an unreliable world, Rosalie's first concern was staying solvent. She warned that fortune could turn, as it had for some of their friends.[69] Even the meticulous Rosalie sometimes had to adjust to a lower income than expected. She had to "confess" to Jules in March 1804, "In spite of my surveillance and my modest and well-administrated home, I did not make any money this term. I only made one hundred louis in six months."[70] The Julliens' revenue came from rented property, a relatively stable source of income.[71] The reason for the lower return was the increased cost of goods. "Everything is so exorbitant!" she exclaimed. "We were drinking old wine from Mâcon. Today we drink new wine that we get for 18 sous a bottle." She quickly added, "Happy are those who have any at all! We do not complain about it. It's nothing."[72] Two weeks later, however, she was willing to complain to Virginie, to whom she wrote, "Our wine makes me recite the [lamentation of the] Jeremiads. We are drinking some new wine, quite rough, for 14 sous a bottle."[73]

Despite the rising cost of goods, frugal spending habits would help her household and Jules's stay afloat. "Economizing is one of the most secure ways to live, and a true fountain of wealth," she professed.[74] When she warned Jules, "You are spending more than you make," she offered a simple solution: "You must lower your expenses!" As Jules had proven to be irresponsible in that regard, she finally suggested that his wife, then nineteen years old and a mother, should manage the purse. "It is within her jurisdiction to maintain order and economize daily. I do not doubt that she will make your home as I make mine," she wrote.[75] In fact, she wrote to Sophie that while she understood the desire to buy books, "buying books takes money, and this good and rich nourishment for the soul does not fill our hungry stomachs. That is why I always return to my eternal soapbox: *wise economizing on everything*."[76]

In addition to controlling expenses, Rosalie advocated hard work. She emphasized the morality that lay behind a good work ethic. She believed that "a man without a job is a body without a soul."[77] She summarized her values in a short description of her neighbor. The Bidaut family lived nearby Rosalie's inherited home in Mantes, outside Paris, where she and Marc-Antoine retreated once in a while. They operated several mills that were a "source of abundance" thanks to the Bidauts' "intelligence and activity." In short, the Bidaut family personified "kindness, vigilance, order, prosperity, [and] simplicity."[78] These qualities helped define the Bidauts as middle-class according to an identity that was increasingly consolidated throughout the mid-eighteenth and early nineteenth centuries.

After the Revolution, Rosalie sounded more and more like an ideal type of a middle-class woman who upheld the virtues of piety, modesty, and even chastity in her family. In her discussions about frugality, hard work, and self-control, Rosalie helped define the bourgeois wife of the nineteenth century. As Garrioch notes, by 1830, the bourgeoisie had articulated values distinct from those above and below them in social status by stressing "their own virtue and moral superiority—expressed in modesty of dress, in sensibility, and in the place of women within the family."[79] The class above them was corrupted by luxury; the class below had taken violence too far during the Revolution. However, Rosalie did not seem to think that the bourgeoisie was already morally superior to other classes because of its values. She had just seen members of her class fail at their effort to create a republic of virtue because they lost their self-control and become too embroiled in internal squabbles. Her son was almost a victim of that failure. If she was part of the process of making the bourgeoisie, it was in the spirit of reform, not pride.[80]

Her much greater concern was more personal. Her family had experienced significant trauma in the mid-1790s. Her desire to regulate diet, take preventive medical measures, safeguard the next generation from danger, and inculcate a spirit of circumspection in her children were part of a reaction to the lack of control she had over her family's fate in the previous decade.

She still worried over the corrupting influence of wealth, and she added to that a concern over power. In 1803, she wrote to Jules, "I never wish for my friends great power or great wealth. I believe, despite the majority opinion, that these two things distance you as much from happiness as from virtue."[81] Furthermore, to aspire to greater wealth was to be ungrateful for the possessions one had. When Jules complained about not being able to afford luxuries, she told him to "thank Providence because you still have the sweetness and joys that three-quarters of our peers do not have."[82] She expressed a similar idea when she explained that she and Marc-Antoine "would be unjust to let ourselves complain [about expenses] because if there is a small minority better off than we, there is a great majority faring far worse."[83] To complain was to ignore the plight of the less fortunate. She felt no moral superiority to the class beneath her.[84]

There was one luxury in which Rosalie was happy to indulge. In 1801, she "obtained a great victory," she told Virginie. "After having asked for it for more than twenty years, I have [Marc-Antoine's] portrait." Rosalie hired an artist to paint his portrait, and hers, not in a particularly grand way or even a very costly one. The small oval portraits, no

Rosalie Jullien was fifty-six and living in Paris when a traveling artist likely drew this portrait. Her gray eyes, the only feature she admired in herself, peer from under a modest bonnet. *Courtesy of the Cabinet des Arts graphiques, Musée Carnavalet, Paris.*

larger than a hand's length, are now in the Musée Carnavalet—in the attic, not on display. They are modest works, but they pleased Rosalie enormously. "Here [Marc-Antoine's portrait] is before my eyes. It is lively and striking. His mouth is open. It looks to me like speech is about to escape his lips."[85]

Her likeness, and that of her husband, also lived on in their children and grandchildren. Not surprisingly, as Rosalie aged she took comfort in thinking about her legacy continuing in the third generation. There was nothing new about her particular attachment to Jules, in whom she saw herself strongly reflected. She had always considered them to have like souls, but toward the end of her life, she also thought more about their physical similarities, emphasizing to a greater degree the continuity of her life through her son. "It seems that I put the best part of myself into you," she told him.[86] And if unfortunately she passed along her "frail" and "poorly organized" body, then at least he drew from her "a strong soul and real courage."[87] She was not deluded about her beauty, recognizing that she had an ordinary face, although she was

Marc-Antoine Jullien was fifty-seven when the same artist drew this portrait. His brow is furrowed in thought, and his mouth is ready to speak, as Rosalie admired. *Courtesy of the Cabinet des Arts graphiques, Musée Carnavalet, Paris.*

proud of her eyes and unabashedly celebrated the fact that some her grandchildren inherited them.[88]

She thought about these things, about her life and about her inevitable death, as she welcomed her grandchildren into the world. Her friends were dying, her cousins as well. No matter the causes, these losses affected her greatly. The passing of a friend "pains me, morally and physically," she told Jules in 1808.[89] She never spoke about death in this way during the Revolution. Something about the context of a post-revolutionary life for Rosalie brought out her mortality. Marc-Antoine died in 1821, after Rosalie's archive of letters ends. They were not always together at the end of their lives. Marc-Antoine, ravaged by his trembles, his headaches, and his insomnia, lived sometimes in their other homes in calmer places than Paris. Rosalie preferred living in the capital and taking retreats occasionally to their home in Pontoise or to visit her grandchildren.

In one of her last letters, she wrote to Jules, "My dear friend, every age has its tastes, its needs, and its pleasures. A moralist like

Jules Jullien inherited his mother's eyes and his father's desire to be a man of letters. His portrait calls attention to his work with educational reformer Pestalozzi and credits him with founding the *Revue Encyclopédic*, a journal that published diverse articles on the arts and sciences. The *Revue* was his main occupation from 1819 to 1830. *Courtesy of the Cabinet des Arts graphiques, Musée Carnavalet, Paris.*

you must know this better than anyone. [Your father and I] are in the confines of our old age. All we need now is peace and tranquility, calm and quiet. Compared to your ardent activity, we are lazy, but we had our time of occupation. And, thank Heaven, we left it behind."[90]

Conclusion

"In Silence and in Shadow"

THE REVOLUTION IS concealed in Rosalie's nineteenth-century letters. Although her children were still pursuing careers in the army, she consciously excluded politics when she wrote. Was her effort to put her world right again after the Revolution akin to erasing the Revolution altogether? If the middle decade of her life was only an anomaly, interrupting the continuity of lifestyle, values, and aspirations of the pre- and postrevolutionary years, did Rosalie have a Revolution at all?

To "have" a revolution suggests experiencing a dramatic and irreversible change. Many historians rightly demonstrate that the Napoleonic Code and other changes in the early nineteenth century put a stop to any gains women had made during the Revolution. The code's preamble declared that the husband was the head of the family, responsible for supervising "the goods and the morals of his companion." Wives and children were legally subordinated to their husbands and fathers. Women required their husbands' consent to own property, plead in court, act as witnesses, or form contracts. If a woman married a foreigner, she lost her French citizenship and was required to live with her husband.[1] Laws complemented the ideology of domesticity, in which a woman's destiny was to be the "mistress of the house."

There is no denying that the category *woman* suffered losses in status at the Revolution's end. But an individual woman's life exists on many scales, including the realms of ideas, laws, environment, friends, family, and individual personality. As the scales contract, Rosalie's particularity increases. In those more intimate spheres of lived experience, the process of ending, surviving, and recovering from a revolution is the most detailed. To find traces of a revolutionized existence, we must look to the places where an individual still had control over her destiny. The world of ideas was men's domain, and men perpetuated the belief that women had gained too much power and destabilized the social order during the Revolution.[2] The world of politics was sealed; public spaces for women also slowly retracted.[3] But Rosalie could control how and with whom she spent her time within the private worlds of friendship and family. She could reshape her daily life and to some degree revise her worldview, values, and identity.

Within those intimate spheres, Rosalie stopped engaging in politics and ceased using the protofeminist language she had developed during the radical years of the Revolution. Many historians believe that in the Old Regime, women were, as Scott puts it, "objects of male obligation" who inspired their husbands to fulfill their social responsibilities. This paradigm helped create passive and active citizenship during the Revolution.[4] Rosalie, however, told Marc-Antoine that his virtue inspired her love and commitment, not the other way around. During the Revolution, she believed women had more virtue than men. But rather than inspire men passively, women actively cast misbehaving men out of the home.[5] After the Revolution, her characterization of women seemed to become extremely passive. She reminded Jules frequently to care for and protect his wife, who possessed the feminine attributes of modesty, chastity, and sensitivity. Her "Emile" had truly found his "Sophie." She supported Rousseauian companionship between Jules and his wife, and it seems that for the first time she also advocated the passive/active paradigm that Rousseau had established. This trend appears to foreshadow the separation of spheres that began in the 1820s, when men and women lived "a world apart."[6]

However, Rosalie wished for men also to leave the public behind. When Jules wrote to her about his desire to advance his career as an author, Rosalie discouraged him from seeking fulfillment outside the family and disparaged men's public roles. She wrote, "Isn't there a wife, a child who have the right to make you happy just as you have the obligation to make them happy? Domestic virtues are the obligatory virtues of men. Public virtues are often illusory virtues, and anyway, one only owes society the virtues that his station requires."[7] She no longer valued public virtue or considered how privately cultivated virtue could affect life outside the family. As a result, women's sphere of influence seems retracted, but the masculine world of politics is unappealing anyway. While rejecting men's public virtues in favor of family obligations, Rosalie encouraged both men and women to prioritize the family, to perfect domestic virtues rather than inauthentic public ones.

Liberty took refuge in the private sphere. There was freedom in domesticity. She told Jules, "There is no real liberty. There is no real contentment in this base world except that which is hidden and locked in the circle of our domestic gods."[8] In Rosalie's postrevolutionary writing, the family became the opposite of the political sphere, which was now corrupted and distanced from its original ideals of 1789. In the nineteenth century, people had control over their happiness only in the home. There, they were free to practice virtue; they took care of each other. As she reflected on a book about a seventeenth-century revolution in Naples (she still enjoyed learning about the places to which Jules traveled), she concluded that, historically, revolutions tended to devolve and fall victim to tyrants. She wrote, "What I observed in *La Révolution*, and what I notice in other books, is that innovators and reformers preach more morality than they follow.... The only virtues I know are domestic."[9] The public virtues that she celebrated during the first five years of the Revolution came home in the nineteenth century. This home was not identical to the sentimental Rousseauist home that the Julliens created before the Revolution, from which good male citizens emerged to form a society. Now, the domestic sphere was the only legitimate space for men and women to practice virtue as they related to each other.

If the home was now the site of all of the ambitions and values that she had once seen protected in the Republic, then her descriptions of women take on new meaning. At the end of a letter in which she told her son how to be a good husband to his wife, she began a reverie on the ideal of motherhood. About Sophie, she wrote, "Look at her, a *mère de famille*. You must think of her always, so dear and so necessary to the world."[10] So necessary why? "Women have this maternal heart that is God's masterpiece. It seems to me that they are called, more than men, to help bring about the interior peace that is the safeguard against corruption."[11] Years after the republican experiment had failed, Rosalie maintained that women had the unique perseverance and position to keep virtue alive in their homes.[12]

Rosalie's trust in women to preserve the values that she saw discarded in public makes sense. She had often defended and celebrated women's place in a republic. It was not women but men who disappointed her, who turned on each other in the Convention, who made war instead of peace. Her disillusionment had begun before Thermidor. As she described her emotional refuges during Year II, she wrote about feminine spaces: nature, her heart, and the home. In May 1794, she explained to Jules, "I propagated republican principles in my child's breast as well as in my friends [amies], in the shadow of the home, a sacred place where women revel in all of their rights, and where all of their duties are marked."[13] This mixture of politics and intimacy is intriguing. Rosalie enjoyed "rights" and taught republicanism in a "sacred" space that was otherwise impenetrable from the outside world of laws and politics. This sacred place was still intact after the Revolution. She wrote to Jules in 1802, "Courage and patience! These are two necessary virtues for almost every man, though few men practice them with the strength that their sex provides. Meanwhile we others, poor women, we practice them in silence and in shadow."[14]

Rosalie had a Revolution while it was under way. There is no question that her gender gave her revolutionary experience its contours and confines. Other revolutionary women encountered those same borders and attempted to cross them. Madame Roland was politically influential through her husband, who became her mouthpiece.[15] Olympe de Gouges self-published a pamphlet that called, among other things, for a completely new understanding of marriage and an acknowledgment of women's distinctive rights within the family.[16] Other unnamed women knit for the soldiers while sitting in the benches at the National Assembly, divorced their husbands or fought for their rightful inheritance, or marched to Versailles on the October Days. All of those actions brought women into contact with the Revolution, either through discourse or through action. In some cases women had impacts on the course of the Revolution; in others they used new laws to their advantage in their private lives.

Rosalie found ways of defining female citizenship that went beyond the highly praised role of Republican Mother. She revolutionized her home by making it the site of political discussions with friends and government leaders. She also left her home to witness Assembly debates, court trials, violent *journées*, and public festivals. She spoke with the sansculottes. She read newspapers. She did not direct Jules, but she mentored him. Most important, she wrote letters.

The process of writing was central to Rosalie's revolutionary experience. She wrote in the privacy of her home in a genre that had long been regarded as appropriate for women.[17] Letter writing itself was not revolutionary.[18] However, the act of writing helped Rosalie refine her political opinions and therefore become a modern woman with a political identity. Writing, according to Carla Hesse, "enables us to separate ourselves from our ideas, to take possession of them, and to exchange them with others across space and time."[19] Correspondence was the medium through which Rosalie constructed a modern self. She created a public persona that participated in the public. Marc-Antoine and Jules almost certainly shared her writing; the leaders she addressed in the Drôme definitely did. The range of Rosalie's revolutionary activity was not grand, but the effects of it on her sense of self and her sense of satisfaction with her inclusion in the Revolution were great. In the privacy of her home, she became an articulate revolutionary and a publicist of republican principles.

Rosalie also had a Revolution in the sense of the lasting impact on her private life once the Revolution was over. Her activities, both public and private, in daylight or in shadow, contributed to revolutionized conceptions of femininity and the family that persisted, although nearly imperceptibly, into the nineteenth century. There is continuity between her political activity during the Revolution and her concentration on domestic life after the Revolution because private spaces were the only spaces where she believed liberty, equality, and fraternity could flourish. The modesty of this remnant of the Revolution should not diminish its significance. It was the only souvenir she kept from a hopeful period after a disappointing finale.

Rosalie represents many women whose interaction with the Revolution took place in privacy, in places that are difficult for historians to glimpse. Components of her story also make her unique among those women. As Jules's mother, she had an unusual connection to the government for several years. Therefore, while Rosalie's life provides insight into forces and experiences that were likely shared by many, the personal details of that life also affected her revolutionary experience profoundly. In turn, her family and its specific background and values influenced the course of the Revolution once Marc-Antoine and Jules were invested with authority. For that reason, personal details, and privacy in general, matter greatly to the history of the Revolution.[20]

Jules valued his mother; he saved all of her letters. But despite the similarities, which Rosalie loved to point out, between him and his mother, he had a different understanding of women. In 1837, he wrote a letter to Simon Lockroy, his son-in-law, husband to his only daughter, Stéphanie. He told Simon how to remedy Stéphanie's boredom and despondency. He wrote, "A good wife always stays busy, either at housework, which takes at least one or two hours a day if she keeps on top of it, or at an art, music, drawing, painting, embroidery, sewing, etc., or at instructive and pleasant reading. Later she will have the sweet and sacred duty of being the *mère de famille.*"[21] Such an ornamental existence was typical for a bourgeois woman in 1837, yet how it contrasts with the example Jules's own mother set for him.

Stéphanie's life was probably very different from her grandmother's, but she shared some similarities with Rosalie. Both witnessed revolutions. Stéphanie saw the establishment of two different republics, the durable Third Republic beginning thirteen years before her death in 1883. Stéphanie also received and wrote many letters. After Sophie died, Jules relied on her for comfort. He wrote to her often. He explained his ideas for articles, complained about how enemies had kept him from fame and fortune, and sent her poems in hopes of receiving her praise. Through her, he learned news from his five sons, who also wrote

Stéphanie dutifully. "You, my dear Stéphanie, you have a noble and saintly mission to fulfill," Jules wrote to her in 1840. "Since the death of your excellent mother, you have become the place of reunion, the center of our family's affection." In the language of Rousseau, he explained, "The women who truly understand their destiny are angels on earth. They wield a sweet and comforting influence on everything that surrounds them. Their weakness is their strength."[22]

Stéphanie inherited her grandmother's letters from her brother Auguste, who had died before he was able to write his father's memoir. She gave them to her only child, Edouard. Rosalie was the first to hold Stéphanie as she entered the world, and Stéphanie was the last person who had known Rosalie to handle her great body of work. It was Stéphanie's children who dedicated Rosalie's tombstone, and they quoted their great-grandmother when they inscribed it, "A mother's heart is the Creator's masterpiece." Whether they understood the political significance that Rosalie had intended when she wrote the same phrase is a mystery. Rosalie died on April 28, 1824, at the age of seventy-eight.

Stéphanie's children also memorialized her, Sophie, Jules, and Marc-Antoine in Père Lachaise. Marc-Antoine's death preceded Rosalie's, on September 27, 1821. His declining health and constant headaches worried his children and grandchildren for many years. He died unexpectedly back home in the Drôme after falling from a window. Some thought it was suicide. Sophie's death followed her mother-in-law's just four days before Christmas in 1832. She was forty-eight years old. Auguste married, had children, and lived in Besançon, where Jules visited him on occasion. Jules died on October 28, 1848, after witnessing three revolutions.

In 1801, Rosalie told Marc-Antoine, "I would rather close my eyes at the edge of an abyss than contemplate its depth. We are all dying from the effects of a Revolution that was conceived to honor men."[23] The extent of her disenchantment is well expressed by the metaphorical abyss. In one of the first letters Rosalie had written to Jules after he went to London in 1792, she began dramatically by recounting a dream she had had about him falling off of a ridge into "an abyss." She told

The Jullien family gravestone is in the Père Lachaise cemetery in Paris. Here lie Marc-Antoine, Rosalie, Jules, Sophie, and Stéphanie. *Photo by author.*

him that she ran down the cliff. She lifted him up and carried him to two men who had followed her cries for help. They reached the top of the abyss at last, "covered in sweat and gasping with pleasure." She declared, "A mother's love gave me the strength of Hercules."[24] Rosalie had many worries in 1792. She worried about her son, about the war, about the success of the Revolution. But she was not worried about her ability to apply all of her strength to saving the things she loved.

In 1803, she had another dream. She wrote to Jules and Sophie about it. "During my long sleepless nights, I think about you, and during my short sleeps, I dream about you," she told them. "How last night's dream would make a beautiful subject in this letter. The terror, the surprise, the tenderness, all the play of the passions were there in such liveliness that I was relieved when I awoke, realizing that it was only a dream." She did not share the dream. "Now that I am awake, I do not want to dream anymore, and I want to talk with you about things other than my nocturnal nonsense."[25]

Rosalie the revolutionary was a brave woman. She walked the edges of many cliffs. As others fell, she survived, and she ensured her family's survival. In her retirement, Rosalie avoided dreams and nonsense. Her sons continued to pursue political careers; they were not daunted by the inconsistency of perpetual revolutions. As Rosalie passed the future on to them, with some hope and measurable concern, she told Jules, "As your father and I are completely retired within our home, we do not know any news except through others and in echoes.... Correspondence is my life."[26] As the echoes grew fainter, her windows closed to the exterior, and her ears filled instead with the scratch of her quill on paper.

APPENDIX

Rosalie's Library

Through Rosalie's direct quotations, passing references, and to some degree her ideas, we can reconstruct part of what was surely a significant library. The following table lists the authors and titles that she mentioned clearly during the period 1785–1810. It is surely not exhaustive.

Time period	Author	Work
Ancient	Homer	*The Odyssey*
	Virgil	*The Aeneid*
	Marcus Aurelius	*Meditations*
	Heraclitus	
	Cicero	
16th century	Montaigne	*On Educating Children*
17th century	Molière	*Le bourgeois gentillhomme*
		Amphytrion
		Les femmes savantes
		Tartuffe
	Cervantes	*Don Quixote*
	La Fontaine	*Fables*
	Madame de Sévigné	*Published letters*
	Milton	*Paradise Lost*
	Racine	*Phèdre*
	Fénelon	
	Pascal	
	Corneille	*Le Compte d'Essex*

(Continued)

(Continued)

Time period	Author	Work
18th century	Richardson	*Clarissa*
		Pamela
		Charles Grandison
	Rousseau	*Emile*
		The Social Contract
		The New Heloise
	Mably	*Entretiens de Phocion*
		Rights and Duties of the Citizen
		Principes de morale
	Swift	*Gulliver's Travels*
	Sterne	*The Life and Opinions of Tristram Shandy, Gentleman*
	Locke	
	Voltaire	*Letters Concerning the English Nation*
		History of Charles XII
	Montesquieu	*Persian Letters*
	Benjamin Franklin	
Unknown		*History of Charles V and Revolutions of Spain*
		History of Italy

Timeline of the French Revolution and the Jullien Family

April 18, 1744	Marc-Antoine Jullien born
September 9, 1745	Rosalie Ducrollay born
April 24, 1769	Marc-Antoine marries Louise Marguerite Metayer
January 22, 1774	Louise Marguerite dies
October 18, 1774	Saint-Cyr Nugues born
March 10, 1775	Jules Jullien born
November 28, 1775	Marc-Antoine's father dies
1777	Rosalie and Marc-Antoine announce their marriage
Spring 1777	Bernard Jullien born, dies sixteen months later
September 1779	Auguste Jullien born
May 5, 1789	Opening of the Estates General
June 20, 1789	Tennis Court Oath
July 14, 1789	Storming of the Bastille
August 26, 1789	National Constituent Assembly adopts the Declaration of the Rights of Man and of the Citizen
October 5–6, 1789	The October Days
July 12, 1790	Civil Constitution of the Clergy
November 27, 1790	Secular clergy required to swear oath to the Constitution
June 20–25, 1791	The king's flight
July 17, 1791	Champ de Mars Massacre
September 13, 1791	Louis XVI signs Constitution, which makes marriage a civil contract
Fall 1791	Jules joins Jacobin Club in Romans
October 1, 1791	Legislative Assembly begins
April 20, 1792	France declares war on Austria

May 1792	Jules leaves for London
June 20, 1792	Popular attack on the Tuileries Palace
July 5, 1792	Assembly declares the *"patrie en danger"*
August 10, 1792	"Second Revolution"
September 2–5, 1792	September Massacres
September 20, 1792	National Convention begins, Marc-Antoine is a member
September 20, 1792	Divorce becomes legal for men and women to pursue equally
September 22, 1792	Establishment of the First Republic
January 21, 1793	Louis XVI executed
March 7, 1793	Beginning of war in the Vendée
March 7, 1793	Equal inheritance among children of both sexes mandated
April 1793	Jules is assistant war commissioner; Rosalie and Marc-Antoine befriend Bertrand Barère
June 2, 1793	Arrest of the Girondins
June 24, 1793	Ratification of the new constitution
June 1793	Rosalie and Marc-Antoine begin meeting socially with Robespierre
July 13, 1793	Charlotte Corday assassinates Jean-Paul Marat
September 17, 1793	Beginning of the Reign of Terror
September 1793	Jules is a traveling agent for the Committee of Public Safety
September 22, 1793	New revolutionary calendar introduced
October 30, 1793	Women's clubs banned
October 31, 1793	Girondist deputies executed
February 1794	Jules denounces Carrier in Nantes
July 27, 1794	9 Thermidor
July 31, 1794	(13 Thermidor) Jules leaves Bordeaux for Paris, unaware of events in the capital, is imprisoned
September 1795	Jules released from prison
1797	Jules joins Bonaparte's army
May 3, 1798	Jules's son born out of wedlock, dies a year later
Spring 1799	Jules arrested in Naples, released a few weeks later.
1801	Jules marries Sophie
1802	Auguste born to Jules and Sophie

1803	Adolphe born to Jules and Sophie
1804	Saint-Cyr born to Jules and Sophie, dies two weeks later
1805	Alfred born to Jules and Sophie
1807	Stéphanie born to Jules and Sophie (other reports indicate 1811)
1811	Alphonse born to Jules and Sophie
1812	Félix born to Jules and Sophie
September 21, 1821	Marc-Antoine dies
April 28, 1824	Rosalie dies
July 1830	July Revolution in France
December 21, 1832	Sophie dies
February 1848	Revolution begins in France
October 28, 1848	Jules dies

Notes

INTRODUCTION

1. R. Jullien to Jullien fils, June 1, 1792, Archives nationales, Paris, 39 AP. All letters cited are from this archive unless otherwise noted. All translations are mine unless otherwise noted.

2. Candice Proctor, in *Women, Equality, and the French Revolution* (New York: Greenwood Press, 1990), traces the dialectic between feminists and anti-feminists and concludes that women's status was worse after the Revolution than before. Madelyn Gutwirth, in *The Twilight of the Goddesses: Women and Representation in the French Revolutionary Era* (New Brunswick, NJ: Rutgers University Press, 1992), explores images of women and their connection to political goals. See also Lisa Beckstrand, *Deviant Women of the French Revolution and the Rise of Feminism* (Madison, NJ: Fairleigh Dickinson University Press, 2009), especially chapter 7, which analyzes the misogynistic rhetoric that accompanied women's executions in 1794.

3. Olwen Hufton, *Women and the Limits of Citizenship in the French Revolution* (Toronto: University of Toronto Press, 1992).

4. Proctor, *Women, Equality, and the French Revolution*, 55.

5. It is helpful to contextualize the ideal of liberty and realize that it can be defined differently. Nancy Hirschmann offers alternative ways for feminist scholars to conceptualize liberty as well as a useful history of eighteenth-century social contract theorists and their competing visions of liberty. See Nancy Hirschmann, *The Subject of Liberty: Toward a Feminist Theory of Freedom* (Princeton, NJ: Princeton University Press, 2003).

6. Joan Landes, *Women and the Public Sphere in the Age of the French Revolution* (Ithaca, NY: Cornell University Press, 1988), 95.

7. The process that preceded that exclusion is documented in Dena Goodman, *The Republic of Letters: A Cultural History of the French Enlightenment* (Ithaca, NY: Cornell University Press, 1994).

8. Lynn Hunt, *The Family Romance of the French Revolution* (Berkeley: University of California Press, 1992).

9. Joan Wallach Scott, *Only Paradoxes to Offer: French Feminists and the Rights of Man* (Cambridge, MA: Harvard University Press, 1996). For a discussion of how women's subordination is fundamental to liberalism, see Carole Pateman, *The Sexual Contract* (Cambridge: Polity Press, 1988).

10. Suzanne Desan, *The Family on Trial in Revolutionary France* (Berkeley: University of California Press, 2004). See also Margaret Darrow, *Revolution in the House: Family, Class, and Inheritance in Southern France, 1775–1825* (Princeton, NJ: Princeton University Press, 1989).

11. Jennifer Heuer, *The Family and the Nation: Gender and Citizenship in Revolutionary France, 1789–1830* (Ithaca, NY: Cornell University Press, 2005).

12. Dominique Godineau, *The Women of Paris and Their French Revolution*, trans. Katherine Streip (Berkeley: University of California Press, 1988).

13. Gita May, *Madame Roland and the Age of Revolution* (New York: Columbia University Press, 1970); Dena Goodman, "Letter Writing and the Emergence of Gendered Subjectivity in Eighteenth-Century France," *Journal of Women's History* 17, no. 2 (2005): 9–37; Siân Reynolds, *Marriage and Revolution: Monsieur and Madame Roland* (Oxford: Oxford University Press, 2012).

14. Scott, *Only Paradoxes to Offer*; John R. Cole, *Between the Queen and the Cabby: Olympe de Gouges's "Rights of Woman"* (New York: McGill-Queen's University Press, 2011).

15. Godineau, *Women of Paris*, 113. Women's political clubs were also significant sites of women's political activity, although Rosalie did not join one. See Olwen Hufton, "Voilà la Citoyenne," *History Today* 39, no. 5 (May 1989): 26–32; and Suzanne Desan, "Constitutional Amazons," in *Re-creating Authority in Revolutionary France*, ed. Bryant T. Ragan Jr. and Elizabeth A. Williams (New Brunswick, NJ: Rutgers University Press, 1992).

16. David Garrioch, *The Formation of the Parisian Bourgeoisie, 1690–1830* (Cambridge: Harvard University Press, 1996), 208.

17. The term *bourgeois* was used in France in Rosalie's lifetime, although its meaning was amorphous. For this reason and others, Sarah Maza contends that there was no such thing as a bourgeoisie at this time. Sarah Maza, *The Myth of the French Bourgeoisie: An Essay on the Social Imaginary, 1750–1850* (Cambridge, MA: Harvard University Press, 2003). Garrioch, however, argues that although "local notables [and] the commercial middle classes" were not uniform in wealth or status, "they were in a sense united by their common exclusion" from positions of power. Garrioch, *Formation of the Parisian Bourgeoisie*, 149, 188. See also David Garrioch, *The Making of Revolutionary Paris* (Berkeley: University of California Press, 2002).

18. Garrioch, *Formation of the Parisian Bourgeoisie*, 7.

19. Robert A. Nye, *Masculinity and Male Codes of Honor in Modern France* (New York: Oxford University Press, 1993), 42.

20. Garrioch, *Formation of the Parisian Bourgeoisie*, 281. Margaret Darrow explains how noblewomen adopted the bourgeois cult of domesticity as well. Margaret Darrow, "French Noblewomen and the New Domesticity, 1750–1850," *Feminist Studies* 5, no. 1 (Spring 1979): 41–65. See also Bonnie G. Smith, *Ladies of the Leisure Class: The Bourgeoises of Northern France in the Nineteenth Century* (Princeton, NJ: Princeton University Press, 1981).

21. There is a lively debate regarding the nature of correspondence in the eighteenth century and how historians should approach it. I have been particularly influenced by Mary McAlpin, *Gender, Authenticity, and the Missive Letter in Eighteenth-Century France: Marie-Anne de La Tour, Rousseau's Real-Life Julie* (Lewisburg, PA: Bucknell University Press, 2006); Janet Gurkin Altman, *Epistolarity: Approaches to a Form* (Columbus: Ohio State University Press, 1982); Mireille Bossis, "Methodological Journeys through Correspondences," *Yale French Studies* 71 (special issue 1986): 643–75; Diaz, *L'épistolaire ou la pensée nomade: Formes et functions de la correspondance dans quelques parcours d'écrivains au XIXe siècle* (Paris: Presses Universitaires de France, 2002); Marie-Claire Grassi, *L'art de la lettre au temps de "La nouvelle Héloïse" et du romantisme* (Geneva: Slatkine, 1994); and Dena Goodman, *Becoming a Woman in the Age of Letters* (Ithaca, NY: Cornell University Press, 2009).

22. For a short biography of Jules, see Robert R. Palmer, *From Jacobin to Liberal: Marc-Antoine Jullien, 1775–1848* (Princeton, NJ: Princeton

University Press, 1993). See also Pierre Gascar, *L'ombre de Robespierre* (Paris: Gallimard, 1979). Gascar's study of Jules's work for the Committee of Public Safety draws on a sample of Rosalie's letters but severely mischaracterizes her personality and her family dynamics. Later in life, Jules wrote on time management, diary keeping, and educational reform; his writings have sparked interest in those fields as well. See Vargas, "L'éducation du 'petit Jullien' agent du Comité de Salut public," in *L'Enfant, la famille et la Révolution française*, ed. Marie-Françoise Lévy (Paris: Olivier Orban, 1990); Lejeune, "Marc-Antoine Jullien: Contrôleur de temps," *Lalies* 28 (2008): 205–20; Jean-Louis Debauve, "A propos de Marc-Antoine Jullien et de la Société polymathique [du Morbihan]," *Bulletin de la Société Polymathique Morbihan, P.-V.* 108 (1981): 43–45; Jean Giraud, "Marc-Antoine Jullien de Paris," *Paedagogica Historica* 15, no. 2 (1975): 379–405; and Helmut Goetz, *Marc-Antoine Jullien de Paris (1775–1848): L'évolution spirituelle d'un révolutionnaire* (Paris: Institut pédagogique national, 1962).

23. Odile Krakovitch, "Un cas de censure familiale: La correspondance revue et corrigée de Rosalie Jullien (1789–1793) [par Edouard Lockroy, son arrière-petit-fils]," *Histoire et Archive* 9 (2001): 81–123; Pierre Vargas, "L'héritage de Marc-Antoine Jullien, de Paris à Moscou," *Annales historiques de la Révolution française* 301 (1995): 409–31; Rosalie Jullien, *Journal d'une bourgeoise pendant la Révolution française*, ed. Edouard Lockroy (Paris: C. Lévy, 1881).

24. Vargas, "L'héritage de Marc-Antoine Jullien." In this article, Vargas references some documents that are not apparently on the microfilm in Romans.

25. Other members of this group include Madame Villé, Madame and Monsieur Sarraillon, and Monsieur Claude Magnan. Marie-Louise Hustache, as part of a master's thesis in 1989 at l'Université Lumière de Lyon 2, under the direction of Pierre Retat, wrote a biography of Ducrollay titled *Une Sévigné chez les Jacobins: Rosalie Jullien*. In 1990, still at the same university and with the same adviser, she received a *diplôme d'études approfondies* for transcribing Ducrollay's correspondence from July 30, 1794, to June 22, 1799. A final resource that the Drôme offers is a private collection of letters from the Nugues family. Their descendants generously permitted me access to their sources, which make their debut in this history and deserve fuller attention in another place.

26. Timothy Tackett has detailed the way that the path to becoming a revolutionary was as individual as the person. Only through a diverse assortment of individual histories can we understand those multiple processes. Timothy Tackett, "Paths to Revolution: The Old Regime Correspondence of Five Future Revolutionaries," *French Historical Studies* 32, no. 4 (Fall 2009): 531–54.

27. Giovanni Levi, "Les usages de la biographie," *Annales: Economies, Sociétés, Civilisations* 6 (November/December 1989): 1325–36; Jill Lepore, "Historians Who Love Too Much: Reflections on Microhistory and Biography," *Journal of American History 88* (2001): 129–44. I have been particularly influenced by Nina Rattner Gelbart, *The King's Midwife: A History and Mystery of Madame du Coudray* (Berkeley: University of California Press, 1998); and Jo Burr Margadant, ed., *The New Biography: Performing Femininity in Nineteenth-Century France* (Berkeley: University of California Press, 2000).

CHAPTER 1

1. R. Jullien to Dubray, Sept. 25, 1784.
2. Olwen Hufton, *The Prospect before Her: A History of Women in Western Europe, 1500–1800* (New York: Vintage Books, 1998), 429.
3. Dena Goodman, "L'Ortografe des Dames: Gender and Language in the Old Regime," *French Historical Studies* 25, no. 2 (2002): 191–223. Rosalie also spelled better than another middle-class French woman whose letters have been studied. Marie de Sérézac "wrote only a few laborious and poorly spelled letters." Christine Adams, *A Taste for Comfort and Status: A Bourgeois Family in Eighteenth-Century France* (University Park: Pennsylvania State University Press, 2000), 7.
4. R. Jullien to Jullien fils, June 18, 1792.
5. R. Jullien to Jullien père, Oct. 1785.
6. R. Jullien to V. Jullien, Jan. 24, 1777.
7. R. Jullien to Jullien fils, June 16, 1792.
8. Archives Communales de Romans-sur-Isère, 61 S27.
9. Archives Départementales de Val d'Oise, 2E15/342.
10. R. Jullien to C. Jullien, June 24, 1787.
11. R. Jullien to V. Jullien, Dec. 30, 1775.

12. Vargas, "L'héritage de Marc-Antoine Jullien," 416.

13. Jean-Louis Flandrin, *Families in Former Times: Kinship, Household and Sexuality*, trans. Richard Southern (New York: Cambridge University Press, 1979), 183.

14. For a discussion of the Church's stance on marriage in this period, see Rosemary O'Day, *The Family and Family Relationships, 1500–1900: England, France, and the United States of America* (New York: St. Martin's Press, 1994), 33–39.

15. For a discussion of the increasing instances of "feeling" being cited in marriage decisions, see Margaret Darrow, "Popular Concepts of Marital Choice in Eighteenth-Century France," *Journal of Social History* 19, no. 2 (Winter 1985): 261–72.

16. Ibid. See also Edward Shorter, "Illegitimacy, Sexual Revolution, and Social Change in Modern Europe," *Journal of Interdisciplinary History* 2, no. 2 (1971): 237–72. As partners strove to create companionate relationships, they blended older patriarchal relationships with the newer forms of unequal but complementary relations. See Goodman, *Becoming a Woman*.

17. R. Jullien to V. Jullien, Dec. 30, 1775.

18. R. Jullien to V. Jullien, Jan. 24, 1777.

19. Ibid.

20. Ibid.

21. R. Jullien to C. Nugues, Sept. 9, 1783, private collection.

22. R. Jullien to Tiberge, Aug. 25, 1779.

23. This form of investment was conservative and reliable. Another bourgeois family made 2,800 livres a year on their rented-out property in 1763, which is approximately the salary of a barrister and half the income of an aristocrat. Adams, *Taste for Comfort*, 57, 68.

24. Ibid., 67–68.

25. R. Jullien to Jullien père, Oct. 12, 1785.

26. R. Jullien to Jullien père, Oct. 30, 1785.

27. R. Jullien to Tiberge, July 10, 1779.

28. R. Jullien to Jullien père, Oct. 30, 1785.

29. R. Jullien to V. Jullien, Jan. 10, 1785.

30. Women's roles in running family businesses were historically integral. Women were especially likely to be bookkeepers. See Louise A. Tilly and Joan W. Scott, *Women, Work, and Family* (New York: Holt, Rinehart and Winston, 1978), especially chapter 3.

31. R. Jullien to Tiberge, July 10, 1779.

32. Roger Pierre et al., *240.000 Drômois: La fin de l'ancien régime les débuts de la Révolution* (Valence: Notre Temps, 1989), 144, 195.

33. R. Jullien to Jullien père, Feb. 1782.

34. R. Jullien to Jullien père, Sept. 2, 1785.

35. R. Jullien to Jullien père, Nov. 14, 1785.

36. Contrast this relationship with those described in Cissie Fairchilds, *Domestic Enemies: Servants and Their Masters in Old Regime France* (Baltimore: Johns Hopkins University Press, 1984). Rosemary O'Day explains that having servants was "widespread throughout the social hierarchy in early modern England, France, and the English American colonies." In place of salary, a servant often received room and board and "all his or her needs—and lived in a style not far below that of the master, mistress and their children." O'Day, *The Family and Family Relationships*, 175, 177.

37. R. Jullien to Dejean, Aug. 15, 1801.

38. R. Jullien to Tiberge, Mar. 25, 1779.

39. Goodman, "Letter Writing and the Emergence of Gendered Subjectivity," 22.

40. Quoted in Marie-Claire Grassi, "Friends and Lovers (or the Codification of Intimacy)," *Yale French Studies* 71 (special issue 1986): 91.

41. Denis Diderot and Claude Yvon, "Friendship," in *The Encyclopedia of Diderot & d'Alembert Collaborative Translation Project*, trans. Jeffrey Merrick (Ann Arbor: MPublishing, University of Michigan Library, 2003), http://hdl.handle.net/2027/spo.did2222.0000.182 (accessed May 1, 2012), originally published as "Amitié," in *Encyclopédie ou Dictionnaire raisonné des sciences, des arts et des métiers* (Paris, 1751), 1:361–62. Indeed, friendship was largely men's domain until approximately 1770, at which time women's letters to each other began to include expressions of endearment similar to those male friends had used since 1700. Grassi, "Friends and Lovers," 84.

42. R. Jullien to Dubray, Mar. 23, 1782.

43. R. Jullien to Tiberge, July 7, 1780. ·

44. Grassi, "Friends and Lovers," 80.

45. Ibid., 81.

46. R. Jullien to Tiberge, Mar. 28, 1780.

47. R. Jullien to Tiberge, Aug. 25, 1779.

48. C. Nugues to Nugues père, Jan. 10, 1784, private collection.
49. R. Jullien to Tiberge, Mar. 25, 1779.
50. R. Jullien to C. Nugues, 1783, private collection.
51. R. Jullien to Tiberge, Mar. 25, 1779.
52. R. Jullien to C. Nugues, July 1, 1780, private collection.
53. C. Nugues to Nugues père, private collection.
54. Jullien fils to S. Nugues, ca. 1784, private collection.
55. S. Nugues to Jullien fils, ca. 1784, private collection.
56. R. Jullien to Jullien fils, Sept. 19, 1785.
57. R. Jullien to Jullien fils, Oct. 20, 1791.
58. R. Jullien to Tiberge, Oct. 5, 1780.
59. R. Jullien to Jullien père, Sept. 1779.
60. R. Jullien to Jullien fils, Oct. 20, 1791.
61. R. Jullien to Jullien père, Sept. 26, 1785.
62. R. Jullien to Jullien père, Oct. 12, 1785.
63. R. Jullien to Jullien père, Nov. 18, 1779.
64. R. Jullien to Jullien fils, Nov. 8, 1785.
65. R. Jullien to Jullien fils, Sept. 29, 1785.
66. R. Jullien to Jullien père, Oct. 1, 1785.
67. Ibid.
68. R. Jullien to Jullien fils, Sept. 29, 1785.
69. R. Jullien to Jullien père, Sept. 17, 1785.
70. R. Jullien to Jullien père, July 16, 1787.
71. R. Jullien to Jullien père, Nov. 13, 1785.
72. Flandrin, *Families in Former Times*, 128.
73. Darrow, "Popular Concepts of Marital Choice."
74. Quoted in Goodman, *Becoming a Woman*, 298–99.
75. R. Jullien to Jullien père, Nov. 18, 1779.
76. R. Jullien to Jullien fils, Oct. 20, 1791.
77. Quoted in Flandrin, *Families in Former Times*, 159.
78. Grassi, "Friends and Lovers," 89.
79. Ibid., 82.
80. R. Jullien to Jullien père, Oct. 23, 1785.

CHAPTER 2

1. R. Jullien to Jullien père, Nov. 14, 1785.
2. On Servan's relationship with the Jullien family, see Palmer, *From Jacobin to Liberal*, 22.

3. Joseph Michel Antoine Servan, *Reflexions sur les Confessions de J. J. Rousseau* (Paris: [H.-E. Vincent], 1783), 15.
4. Jullien père to J. Servan, Sept. 29, 1781, Archives Communales de Romans-sur-Isère, 61 S27.
5. For comparison, see Robert Darnton, *The Great Cat Massacre and Other Episodes in French Cultural History* (New York: Vintage Books, 1984), especially chapter 6.
6. She referenced, for example, Pascal, Muhammad, Confucius, and Numa. R. Jullien to Jullien père, Oct. 30, 1785.
7. J. Servan to Jullien père, Apr. 1776, Archives Communales de Romans-sur-Isère, 61 S27.
8. J. Servan to Jullien père, 1782, Archives Communales de Romans-sur-Isère, 61 S27.
9. J. Servan to Jullien père, June 17, 1781, Archives Communales de Romans-sur-Isère, 61 S27.
10. J. Servan to Jullien père, May 3, 1782, Archives Communales de Romans-sur-Isère, 61 S27.
11. Ibid.
12. J. Servan to Jullien père, June 17, 1781, Archives Communales de Romans-sur-Isère, 61 S27.
13. Jullien père to J. Servan, Sept. 29, 1781, Archives Communales de Romans-sur-Isère, 61 S25.
14. Ibid.
15. Quoted in Darnton, *Great Cat Massacre*, 236.
16. R. Jullien to Jullien fils, June 16, 1792.
17. Keith Michael Baker, "A Script for a French Revolution: The Political Consciousness of the Abbé Mably," *Eighteenth-Century Studies* 14, no. 3 (Spring 1981): 235–63.
18. See Sarah Maza, *Private Lives and Public Affairs: The Causes Célèbres of Prerevolutionary France* (Berkeley: University of California Press, 1993).
19. Baker, "Script for a French Revolution," 262.
20. Quoted in Keith Michael Baker, *Inventing the French Revolution: Essays on French Political Culture in the Eighteenth Century* (Cambridge: Cambridge University Press, 1990), 103.
21. Mably to Jullien père, July 9, 1768, Archives Communales de Romans-sur-Isère, 61 S27.
22. Norman Hampson, "Mably and the Montagnards," *French History* 16, no. 4 (2002): 408. Hampson suggests that sometimes speakers who seemed to

be quoting Rousseau were actually referencing Mably. "Both [Rousseau and Mably] agreed that the essential object of politics was the creation of a collective moral order, which they thought had been exemplified in republican Rome and especially in Sparta. There was a common ground between Rousseau's conception of a general will which was a moral imperative for every individual and Mably's belief that what he called 'reason' was part of some Providential natural order. Both were insistent that this was not to be confused with the *volonté de tous*, or what people thought they wanted" (ibid.).

23. R. Jullien to Jullien père, Dec. 5, 1785.
24. Jean-Jacques Rousseau, *Emile*, trans. by Barbara Foxley, http://www.gutenberg.org/ebooks/5427, book I.
25. Penny Weiss and Anne Harper, "Rousseau's Political Defense of the Sex-Roled Family," in *Feminist Interpretations of Jean-Jacques Rousseau*, ed. Lynda Lange (University Park: Pennsylvania State University Press, 2002), 69.
26. Rousseau, *Emile*, book I.
27. Weiss and Harper, "Rousseau's Political Defense," 51; George D. Sussman, *Selling Mothers' Milk: The Wet-Nursing Business in France, 1715–1914* (Urbana: University of Illinois Press, 1982), 20.
28. Nina Gelbart associates this concern with a midwife's success at getting a government pension to teach safer delivery techniques. Gelbart, *The King's Midwife*.
29. Sussman, *Selling Mothers' Milk*, 67.
30. Londa Schiebinger, "Why Mammals Are Called Mammals: Gender Politics in Eighteenth-Century Natural History," *American Historical Review* 98, no. 2 (April 1993): 382–411.
31. R. Jullien to Jullien fils, Oct. 20, 1791.
32. R. Jullien to V. Jullien, Jan. 24, 1777.
33. R. Jullien to V. Jullien, ca. 1777.
34. R. Jullien to Tiberge, Feb. 7, 1781.
35. Lynda Lange, "Rousseau and Modern Feminism," in *Feminist Interpretations of Jean-Jacques Rousseau*, ed. Lynda Lange (University Park: Pennsylvania State University Press, 2002), 34.
36. Quoted in Goodman, *Becoming a Woman*, 330.
37. R. Jullien to Jullien père, Nov. 22, 1784.

38. R. Jullien to Jullien père, Sept. 12, 1785. As always in their letters, they again placed the beginning of their marriage in 1775.
39. Rousseau, *Emile*, book V.
40. Proctor, *Women, Equality, and the French Revolution*, 8. Marisa Linton explains that sources other than Rousseau also influenced popular conceptions of female virtue. The Christian ideal emphasized passive suffering; the Roman emphasized loyalty to husband and children. Marisa Linton, "Virtue Rewarded? Women and the Politics of Virtue in 18th-Century France. Part I," *History of European Ideas* 26, no. 1 (2000): 36, 41.
41. Quoted in Goodman, *Becoming a Woman*, 302.
42. R. Jullien to Jullien père, Oct. 5, 1785.
43. R. Jullien to Dejean, Mar. 23, 1782.
44. R. Jullien to Tiberge, Oct. 5, 1780.
45. William Reddy describes *Pamela* in terms of sentimentalism: "(1) that superior virtue is linked to simplicity, openness, and lowly rank, because virtue is an outgrowth of natural sentiments we all share; (2) that women are more likely to develop such virtue; (3) that men are more likely to be enslaved to their stronger passions; (4) that true beauty lies in virtuous innocence and sincerity; (5) that reading (especially novels) and writing are important instruments for the cultivation of sensitivity and virtue; (6) that romantic attachment is the proper foundation of marriage; and (7) that a marriage so founded is both a refuge and a school of virtue." William M. Reddy, *The Navigation of Feeling: A Framework for the History of Emotions* (Cambridge: Cambridge University Press, 2001), 158.
46. R. Jullien to Jullien père, Oct. 23, 1785. She also read and sometimes referenced another popular volume, a collection of letters by Madame de Sévigné from the seventeenth century. See Michèle Longino Farrell, *Performing Motherhood: The Sévigné Correspondence* (Cambridge, MA: University Press of New England, 1991); and Janet Gurkin Altman, "The Letter Book as a Literary Institution 1539–1789: Toward a Cultural History of Published Correspondences in France," *Yale French Studies* 71 (special issue 1986): 17–62. See also my discussion of Rosalie's publishing aspirations: Lindsay Holowach, "L'éveil d'une conscience féminine au cours de la Revolution française: Rosalie Jullien (1785–1792)," in *Colloque Archive epistolaire et Histoire*, ed. Mireille Bossis and Lucia Bergamasco (Paris: Connaissances et Savoirs, 2007).

47. "A woman's power lay in her virtue. This was the source of her *empire*, that illusive eighteenth-century concept of female influence or even dominance. It was the tyranny of the weak over the strong. 'Her orders are caresses, her menaces are tears,' said Rousseau." Proctor, *Women, Equality, and the French Revolution*, 12.

48. R. Jullien to Jullien père, Oct. 23, 1785.

49. R. Jullien to Tiberge, July 10, 1779.

50. R. Jullien to L. Dubray, Mar. 23, 1782.

51. R. Jullien to Jullien père, Oct. 23, 1785.

52. R. Jullien to Jullien fils, Sept. 4, 1791.

53. R. Jullien to Jullien père, Oct. 23, 1785.

54. R. Jullien to Jullien fils, Sept. 29, 1785.

55. R. Jullien to Jullien père, Oct. 30, 1785.

56. Ibid.

57. R. Jullien to Jullien père, Oct. 23, 1785.

58. R. Jullien to Jullien père, Oct. 17, 1785.

59. R. Jullien to Jullien père, Sept. 17, 1785.

60. R. Jullien to Jullien père, Oct. 10, 1785.

61. R. Jullien to Tiberge, Oct. 5, 1780.

62. John Shovlin, *The Political Economy of Virtue: Luxury, Patriotism, and the Origins of the French Revolution* (Ithaca, NY: Cornell University Press, 2006), 17. This concern about luxury was probably not new to Rosalie, as a discourse had existed since the mid-eighteenth century and was shared by provincial nobles and notables and the "middling elite," according to Shovlin (ibid., 38).

63. Ibid., 38–39.

64. Adams, *Taste for Comfort*, 31.

65. R. Jullien to Jullien père, Oct. 23, 1785.

66. R. Jullien to Jullien fils, Sept. 19, 1785.

67. R. Jullien to Jullien père, Dec. 5, 1785.

68. It is that phenomenon, of an ambitious middle-class Rousseauian wishing to cast off the restraints imposed by privilege under the old order, that suggests to R. R. Palmer that Jules's history is one of class conflict. Palmer, *From Jacobin to Liberal*, 54.

69. Revisionist historians have sought to replace the Marxist interpretation of the origins of the Revolution with an explanation that relies not on material circumstances but on the influence of ideas. Leaders in

this interpretation include Baker, *Inventing the French Revolution*; and François Furet, *Interpreting the French Revolution*, trans. Elborg Forster (Paris: Editions de la Maison des Sciences de l'Homme, 1988). For other accounts of the cultural origins of the Revolution, see Roger Chartier, *The Cultural Origins of the French Revolution*, trans. Lydia G. Cochrane (Durham, NC: Duke University Press, 1991); and Margaret Jacob, *Living the Enlightenment: Freemasonry and Politics in Eighteenth-Century Europe* (New York: Oxford University Press, 1991).

70. Robert Darnton, "The High Enlightenment and the Low Life of Literature," *Past and Present* 51 (1971): 95.

71. Marc-Antoine was not a member of the Constituent Assembly, but it is enlightening to compare him to those who were, as he was an active revolutionary in clubs and would eventually be a member of the Convention. Timothy Tackett found that 10 deputies were philosophes, 60 (or 4 percent) were member of learned academies, 20 percent were members of Masonic lodges, 16 were Mesmerists, and 116 had published something (mostly letters, history, politics, and law). Timothy Tackett, *Becoming a Revolutionary: The Deputies of the French National Assembly and the Emergence of a Revolutionary Culture (1789–1790)* (Princeton, NJ: Princeton University Press, 1996).

CHAPTER 3

1. Tackett, *When the King Took Flight* (Cambridge, MA: Harvard University Press, 2003); David Jordan, *The King's Trial: The French Revolution vs. Louis XVI* (Berkeley: University of California Press, 1979); Paul Hanson, *The Jacobin Republic under Fire: The Federalist Revolt in the French Revolution* (University Park: Pennsylvania State University Press, 2003).

2. R. Jullien to Jullien père, Aug. 27, 1789.

3. See Georges Lefebvre, *The Coming of the French Revolution*, trans. R. R. Palmer (Princeton, NJ: Princeton University Press, 1975).

4. R. Jullien to Jullien père, Aug. 27, 1789.

5. Ibid.

6. Ibid.

7. Ibid.

8. Ibid.

9. R. Jullien to Jullien père, Sept. 1, 1789.

10. Ibid.

11. Ibid.

12. Ibid.

13. R. Jullien to Jullien père, Sept. 10, 1789.

14. R. Jullien to Jullien père, Sept. 22, 1789.

15. Ibid.

16. Olwen Hufton explains the continuity between Old Regime traditions of women protesting food shortages and their actions during the October Days. David Garrioch argues that the October Days signaled a new era in women's activism because women were acting more politically than ever before. Jean-Clément Martin sees the October Days as the beginning of the feminization of the *peuple*. Hufton, *Women and the Limits of Citizenship*, 7–12; David Garrioch, "The Everyday Lives of Parisian Women and the October Days of 1789," *Social History* 24, no. 3 (October 1999): 231–49; Jean-Clément Martin, *La révolte brisée: Femmes dans la Révolution française et l'Empire* (Paris: Armand Colin, 2008).

17. R. Jullien to Jullien père, Oct. 5, 1789.

18. For details on crowd mobilization, see George Rudé, *The Crowd in the French Revolution* (Oxford: Clarendon Press, 1959).

19. R. Jullien to Jullien père, Oct. 5, 1789.

20. Ibid.

21. R. Jullien to V. Jullien, Apr. 14, 1790. Regarding the Troglodytes, see Charles de Secondat baron de Montesquieu, *The Persian Letters*, trans. Margaret Mauldon (New York: Oxford University Press, 2008), 15–22.

22. R. Jullien to V. Jullien, Apr. 14, 1790.

23. R. Jullien to V. Jullien, Apr. 18, 1790.

24. R. Jullien to V. Jullien, Apr. 14, 1790.

25. Ibid.

26. S. Nugues to Nugues père, July 29, 1790, private collection.

27. R. Jullien to Jullien fils, Oct. 6, 1791.

28. R. Jullien to Jullien fils, Oct. 21, 1791.

29. See Timothy Tackett, "Conspiracy Obsession in a Time of Revolution: French Elites and the Origins of the Terror, 1789–1792," *American Historical Review* 105, no. 3 (June 2000): 691–713.

30. Mita Choudhury, *Convents and Nuns in Eighteenth-Century French Politics and Culture* (Ithaca, NY: Cornell University Press, 2004).

31. Ibid., 180.

32. See Hufton, *Women and the Limits of Citizenship*, especially chapter 2.
33. Timothy Tackett, *Priest and Parish in Eighteenth-Century France* (Princeton, NJ: Princeton University Press, 1977), 272.
34. Ibid., 143.
35. Ibid., 261–63.
36. Ibid., 277.
37. Ibid., 281.
38. Ibid.
39. Tackett, *Becoming a Revolutionary*, 267–68.
40. R. Jullien to V. Jullien, Apr. 14, 1790.
41. R. Jullien to Jullien fils, Sept. 28, 1791.
42. Tackett, *When the King Took Flight*. For a discussion of attitudes toward the king, see John Markoff, "Images of the King at the Beginning of the Revolution," in *Revolutionary Demands: A Content Analysis of the Cahiers de Doléances of 1789*, ed. Gilbert Shapiro and John Markoff, 369–76 (Stanford, CA: Stanford University Press, 1997).
43. R. Jullien to Jullien père, Aug. 14, 1791.
44. R. Jullien to Jullien père, June 1, 1790.
45. R. Jullien to Jullien fils, Aug. 11, 1791.
46. R. Jullien to Jullien fils, Sept. 4, 1791.
47. R. Jullien to Jullien père, August 14, 1791.
48. R. Jullien to Jullien fils, Aug. 11, 1791.
49. Ibid.
50. R. Jullien to Jullien fils, Aug. 14, 1791.
51. Jeremy Popkin, *Revolutionary News: The Press in France, 1789–1799* (Durham, NC: Duke University Press, 1990).
52. R. Jullien to Jullien fils, Aug. 11, 1791.
53. Ibid.
54. R. Jullien to Jullien fils, Aug. 20, 1791.
55. Darlene Levy describes 1791 as "a period of rapid radicalization, when definitions of the sovereign nation and the location of its general will were fiercely and continuously contested, all meanings of French revolutionary citizenship, along with the ideologies attached to them, were plural and unstable, marked by complex internal tensions and fissures." Female citizenship, whatever it was to be, was similarly in flux at this time. Darlene Gay Levy, "Women's Revolutionary Citizenship in Action, 1791: Setting the Boundaries," in *The French Revolution and the Meaning of Citizenship*,

ed. Renée Waldinger, Philip Dawson, and Isser Woloch (Westport, CT: Greenwood Press, 1993), 182.

56. R. Jullien to Jullien fils, Aug. 20, 1791.
57. R. Jullien to Jullien père, Aug. 14, 1791.
58. R. Jullien to Jullien fils, Aug. 20, 1791.
59. R. Jullien to Jullien père, Aug. 14, 1791.
60. Ibid.
61. Tackett, "Paths to Revolution," 536.
62. Ibid., 550.
63. R. Jullien to Jullien fils, Aug. 25, 1791. For analysis of the effects of festivals, see Mona Ozouf, *Festivals and the French Revolution*, trans. Alan Sheridan (Cambridge, MA: Harvard University Press, 1988).
64. R. Jullien to Jullien fils, Sept. 24, 1791.
65. R. Jullien to Jullien fils, Aug. 20, 1791.

CHAPTER 4

1. R. Jullien to Jullien fils, May 19, 1792.
2. Georges Brunel, *La poste à Paris depuis sa creation jusqu'à mos jours, etude historique et anecdotique* (Amiens: Yvert & Teller, 1920), 33–34, 104–5.
3. R. Jullien to Jullien père, Aug. 25, 1792.
4. For a discussion of French nationalism and English relations, see David Bell, *The Cult of the Nation in France: Inventing Nationalism, 1680–1800* (Cambridge, MA: Harvard University Press, 2001).
5. Archives nationales, Paris, 39 AP, 3.
6. R. Jullien to Jullien fils, Oct. 20, 1791.
7. R. Jullien to Jullien fils, June 1, 1792.
8. R. Jullien to Jullien père, May 28, 1792.
9. R. Jullien to Jullien père, May 16, 1792. The letters were meant to introduce him to Joseph Priestly, among others.
10. R. Jullien to Jullien fils, June 16, 1792.
11. S. Nugues to Jullien fils, Feb. 15, 1794.
12. Arno Mayer, *The Furies: Violence and Terror in the French and Russian Revolutions* (Princeton, NJ: Princeton University Press, 2000). See also Jean-Clément Martin, *Contre-révolution, révolution et nation en France: 1789–1799* (Paris: Editions du Seuil, 1998).
13. Tackett, "Conspiracy Obsession." For an analysis of the dynamics between revolutionary and counterrevolutionary forces, see Hanson, *The Jacobin Republic under Fire;* and Martin, *Contre-révolution, révolution et nation.*

14. R. Jullien to Jullien père, May 23, 1791.
15. Georges Lefebvre connects the popular revolution in part to fear of an aristocratic conspiracy. Lefebvre, *The Coming of the French Revolution*, 119.
16. Analyses of the role of the people of Paris in the Revolution include a sympathetic look by Albert Soboul in *The Parisian Sans-Culottes and the French Revolution 1793–4*, trans. Gwynne Lewis (Oxford: Clarendon Press, 1964). See also Godineau, *Women of Paris*; and Hufton, *Women and the Limits of Citizenship*.
17. R. Jullien to Jullien père, May 16, 1792.
18. R. Jullien to Jullien père, June 19, 1792.
19. Ibid.
20. R. Jullien to Jullien fils, July 26, 1792.
21. R. Jullien to Jullien fils, July 10, 1792.
22. R. Jullien to Jullien fils, July 26, 1792.
23. R. Jullien to Jullien fils, July 18, 1792.
24. R. Jullien to Jullien fils, June 26, 1792.
25. R. Jullien to Jullien fils, July 10, 1792.
26. R. Jullien to Jullien fils, July 18, 1792.
27. R. Jullien to Jullien père, June 24, 1792.
28. R. Jullien to Jullien fils, June 26, 1792.
29. R. Jullien to Jullien père, June 24, 1792.
30. R. Jullien to Jullien père, June 30, 1792.
31. R. Jullien to Jullien fils, Aug. 4, 1792; R. Jullien to Jullien père, Aug. 5, 1792.
32. R. Jullien to Jullien père, June 24, 1792.
33. R. Jullien to Jullien fils, Aug. 4, 1792.
34. R. Jullien to Jullien père, Aug. 5, 1792.
35. The first mention of her being at the National Assembly is in R. Jullien to Jullien père, May 23, 1792. She called the Assembly beautiful and interesting a few days later; R. Jullien to Jullien fils, May 28, 1792.
36. R. Jullien to Jullien fils, July 10, 1792.
37. R. Jullien to Jullien père, Aug. 5, 1792.
38. R. Jullien to Jullien fils, Aug. 8, 1792.
39. R. Jullien to V. Jullien, Aug. 9, 1792.
40. R. Jullien to Jullien père, Aug. 10, 1792.
41. Ibid.
42. R. Jullien to Jullien fils, Aug. 21, 1792.
43. R. Jullien to Jullien père, Aug. 15, 1792.

44. R. Jullien to Jullien fils, Aug. 27, 1792.

45. R. Jullien to Jullien père, Aug. 22, 1792.

46. R. Jullien to Jullien fils, Aug. 18, 1792.

47. R. Jullien to Jullien père, Aug. 7, 1792.

48. R. Jullien to Jullien fils, Aug. 8, 1792.

49. R. Jullien to Jullien fils, Aug. 18, 1792.

50. R. Jullien to Jullien fils, Aug. 10 and 27, 1792.

51. R. Jullien to Jullien fils, Aug. 27, 1792.

52. R. Jullien to Jullien père, Aug. 30, 1792.

53. R. Jullien to Jullien fils, Aug. 18, 1792.

54. R. Jullien to Jullien père, Aug. 25, 1792.

55. R. Jullien to Jullien fils, Aug. 18, 1792.

56. R. Jullien to Jullien père, Aug. 26, 1792.

57. R. Jullien to Jullien fils, June 8, 1792.

58. R. Jullien to Jullien père, Sept. 2, 1792.

59. Ibid.

60. Ibid.

61. R. Jullien to Jullien fils, Sept. 6, 1792.

62. R. Jullien to Jullien père, Sept. 3, 1792.

63. R. Jullien to Jullien fils, Oct. 24, 1792.

64. R. Jullien to Jullien fils, May 28 and July 18, 1792.

65. R. Jullien to Jullien fils, June 1, 1792.

66. R. Jullien to Jullien père, Aug. 15, 1792.

67. R. Jullien to Jullien père, June 14, 1792.

68. R. Jullien to Jullien fils, June 8, 1792.

69. *Archives Parlementaires DE 1787 à 1860 recueil complet*, vol. 52 (Paris, 1897), 570.

70. Ibid.

71. He also came out in favor of trying the king. Marc-Antoine "was one of the first to speak in the Convention when the trial of the king began. Agreeing with Robespierre, he excitedly insisted that Louis XVI was a 'monster' who deserved no constitutional protection, that he himself would have put him to death immediately on 10 August, and that France should set an example to Europe of how kings should be dealt with." Palmer, *From Jacobin to Liberal*, 24.

72. R. Jullien to Jullien père, May 3, 1792.

73. R. Jullien to Jullien fils, June 8 and 23, 1792.

74. R. Jullien to Jullien fils, June 1, 1792.
75. R. Jullien to Jullien fils, May 19, 1792. Readers may be interested in what Rosalie had to say about the slave revolts in Haiti and subsequent abolition of slavery. In fact, she said nothing, although she did send her regards to Manlius, the *"joli nègre"* who accompanied Jules on his mission when he was assistant war commissioner in the summer of 1793.
76. R. Jullien to Jullien fils, June 1, 1792.
77. R. Jullien to Jullien fils, May 19, 1792.
78. R. Jullien to Jullien fils, June 23, 1792.
79. R. Jullien to Jullien fils, June 1, 1792.
80. R. Jullien to Jullien fils, June 26, 1792.
81. R. Jullien to Jullien fils, May 19, 1792.
82. R. Jullien to Jullien fils, Aug. 25, 1792.
83. R. Jullien to Jullien père, June 14, 1792.
84. R. Jullien to Jullien père, June 19, 1792.
85. Lindsay A. H. Parker, "Family and Feminism in the French Revolution: The Case of Rosalie Ducrollay Jullien," *Journal of Women's History* 24, no. 3 (Fall 2012): 39–61.
86. R. Jullien to Jullien père, Aug. 30, 1792.
87. R. Jullien to Jullien père, Sept. 1, 1792.
88. R. Jullien to Jullien père, Apr. 30, 1792.
89. Ibid.
90. R. Jullien to V. Jullien, Aug. 9, 1792.
91. R. Jullien to Jullien fils, Oct. 17, 1792.
92. R. Jullien to Jullien père, June 14, 1792.

CHAPTER 5

1. Palmer, *From Jacobin to Liberal*, 22.
2. R. Jullien to Jullien fils, Apr. 2, 1793.
3. Partly for this reason, Lynn Hunt interprets the Revolution as a "family romance" in which brothers assassinated their father-king. Hunt, *Family Romance*.
4. Heuer, *The Family and the Nation*, 45, 86–98.
5. Hanson, *The Jacobin Republic under Fire*, 57.
6. Tackett, "Conspiracy Obsession," 706.
7. Hanson, *The Jacobin Republic under Fire*, 237.

8. Ibid., 34.
9. The Mountain "only wants one king: the law," she explained. R. Jullien to Jullien fils, Apr. 16, 1793.
10. Marisa Linton, "Fatal Friendships: The Politics of Jacobin Friendship," *French Historical Studies* 31, no. 1 (Winter 2008): 54.
11. Ibid., 65.
12. R. Jullien to Jullien fils, Apr. 2, 1793.
13. R. Jullien to Jullien fils, Apr. 16 and 23, 1793.
14. R. Jullien to Jullien fils, May 19, 1793.
15. R. Jullien to Jullien fils, May 2, 1793.
16. R. Jullien to Jullien fils, May 14, 1793.
17. R. Jullien to Jullien fils, May 28, 1793.
18. R. Jullien to Jullien fils, July 7, 1793.
19. R. Jullien to Jullien fils, July 21, 1793.
20. R. Jullien to Jullien père, Aug. 14, 1791.
21. R. Jullien to Jullien père, June 14, 1792.
22. R. Jullien to Jullien fils, June 16, 1792. Jean Robiquet cites a letter from *Journal d'une Bourgeoise*, a collection of letters published by Rosalie's great-grandson, which indicates that Robespierre and his sister had dinner with Rosalie in August 1792. That letter, however, is not in the National Archives, and the content Robiquet cites is perhaps a result of editing on Edouard Lockroy's part. Jean Robiquet, *Daily Life in the French Revolution*, trans. James Kirkup (New York: Macmillan, 1965). Robiquet's account is questionable because of his comparison of "modest" Rosalie and "pompous" Madame Roland (113).
23. R. Jullien to Jullien fils, June 20, 1793. The 1793 Constitution allowed universal male suffrage and proclaimed the people to be the source of sovereignty.
24. R. Jullien to Jullien fils, June 25, 1793.
25. R. Jullien to Jullien fils, Jan. 6, 1794.
26. R. Jullien to Jullien fils, Dec. 18, 1793. Jean-Pierre Gross also notes that the Jacobin government did several positive things for the French, including food and land redistribution, progressive taxation, work programs, and educational reform. He argues that "ideological prudence...stands in marked contrast to the boldness of [the Committee members'] language." Jean-Pierre Gross, *Fair Shares for All: Jacobin Egalitarianism in Practice* (New York: Cambridge University Press, 1997), 23.

27. R. Jullien to Jullien fils, Apr. 18, 1793.

28. R. Jullien to Jullien fils, May 16, 1793.

29. R. Jullien to Jullien fils, May 26, 1793.

30. Archives Communales de Romans-sur-Isère, 61 S.

31. Ibid.

32. Palmer, *From Jacobin to Liberal*, 31.

33. Ibid., 9.

34. R. Jullien to Jullien fils, Oct. 5, 1793.

35. Palmer, *From Jacobin to Liberal*. See also Robert R. Palmer, *Twelve Who Ruled: The Year of Terror in the French Revolution* (Princeton, NJ: Princeton University Press, 1941), 222–24; and Gascar, *L'ombre de Robespierre*.

36. Quoted in Palmer, *From Jacobin to Liberal*, 44.

37. S. Nugues to R. Jullien, Sept. 19, 1793.

38. R. Jullien to Jullien fils, Oct. 27, 1793.

39. Quoted in Palmer, *Twelve Who Ruled*, 223.

40. R. Jullien to Jullien fils, Feb. 11, 1794.

41. R. Jullien to Jullien fils, Feb. 17, 1794.

42. R. Jullien to Procurer General Payan, June 24, 1793.

43. R. Jullien to Jullien fils, Feb. 27, 1794.

44. Ibid.

45. Ibid. See also Hampson, "Mably and the Montagnards," 407–8.

46. R. Jullien to Jullien fils, Feb. 11, 1794.

47. R. Jullien to Jullien fils, Dec. 18, 1793.

48. R. Jullien to Jullien fils, Feb. 27, 1794.

49. Hufton, *Women and the Limits of Citizenship*, 49. More recent researchers have viewed the closing of women's clubs as a more complex issue. Jennifer Heuer notes that men's political activity was also restricted during Year II. Heuer, *The Family and the Nation*, 50, 85.

50. R. Jullien to Payan, June 24, 1793.

51. Godineau, *Women of Paris*, 122.

52. R. Jullien to Jullien fils, Apr. 29, 1793.

53. Another example of this logic comes from Marie Madeleine Jodin, who wrote a treatise in 1790 titled *Legislative View for Women*, which asked the Constituent Assembly for "the elimination of public prostitution, for the setting-up of a women's legislature with a jurisdiction over women in relation to family disputes, for the abolition of the *police des moeurs* (morals police), for the establishment of workshops

and hostels for indigent women, and for the institution of the right to divorce." She "resolve[d] the issue of women's capacity for entering public life by identifying with their role as mothers—both to their families and to society, in the same way as paternal authority flowed from the king/state to the father/ family." Felicia Gordon, "The Gendered Citizen: Marie Madeleine Jodin (1741–90)," in *The French Experience from the Republic to Monarchy, 1792–1824: New Dawns in Politics, Knowledge and Culture*, ed. Máire F. Cross and David Williams (New York: Palgrave, 2000), 12, 18.

54. R. Jullien to Jullien fils, Sept. 16, 1793.

55. Heuer, *The Family and the Nation*, 38.

56. Godineau, *Women of Paris*, 134.

57. R. Jullien to Jullien fils, July 8, 1793.

58. R. Jullien to Jullien fils, Sept. 30, 1793.

59. R. Jullien to Jullien fils, Nov. 4, 1793.

60. R. Jullien to Jullien fils, Nov. 18, 1793.

61. R. Jullien to Jullien fils, Feb. 24, 1794.

62. R. Jullien to Jullien fils, Sept. 30, 1793.

63. R. Jullien to Jullien fils, Nov. 1, 1793.

64. R. Jullien to Jullien fils, Jan. 1, 1794.

65. R. Jullien to Jullien fils, Feb. 27, 1794. This type of language has been found in other correspondence as well. See Nye, *Masculinity and Male Codes of Honor*, 34.

66. R. Jullien to Jullien fils, Feb. 24, 1794.

67. R. Jullien to Jullien fils, Feb. 27, 1794.

68. R. Jullien to Jullien fils, Jan. 1, 1794.

69. R. Jullien to Jullien fils, Apr. 16, 1793.

70. R. Jullien to Jullien fils, Sept. 21, 1793.

71. Pierre Vargas notes that Rosalie discussed *le peuple* and the nation with familial language. Vargas, "L'éducation du 'petit Jullien,'" 233.

72. R. Jullien to Jullien fils, Jan. 29, 1794.

73. R. Jullien to Jullien fils, Nov. 9, 1793.

CHAPTER 6

1. R. Jullien to Jullien père, Mar. 31, 1785.

2. R. Jullien to Jullien fils, Apr. 9, 1794.

3. In 1791, decapitation was declared to be the only permitted form of capital punishment. This reflected a desire to treat all accused criminals equally. On March 30, 1792, the Legislative Assembly decided the guillotine would be the only method approved for execution.

4. Dorinda Outram also sees class as an element in the relationship between victim and audience. The victims wanted to appear self-possessed to the lower-class audience, which resulted in a lack of drama. Dorinda Outram, *The Body and the French Revolution: Sex, Class and Political Culture* (New Haven, CT: Yale University Press, 1989), 114–15, 123.

5. R. Jullien to Jullien fils, Oct. 26, 1793.

6. R. Jullien to Jullien père, Nov. 4, 1793.

7. R. Jullien to Jullien fils, Nov. 1, 1793.

8. R. Jullien to Jullien fils, Sept. 30, 1793.

9. Ibid.

10. Ibid.

11. Furet, *Interpreting the French Revolution*, 77.

12. Reddy, *Navigation of Feeling*, 127, 259.

13. R. Jullien to Jullien fils, Sept. 30, 1793.

14. R. Jullien to Jullien fils, Dec. 18, 1793.

15. R. Jullien to Jullien fils, Jan. 29, 1794.

16. Reddy, *Navigation of Feeling*, 290.

17. Ibid., 203.

18. Ibid., 290.

19. Jan Goldstein also notes this shift as part of the process of making the "post-revolutionary self." Jan Goldstein, *The Post-revolutionary Self: Politics and Psyche in France, 1750–1850* (Cambridge, MA: Harvard University Press, 2005).

20. R. Jullien to Jullien fils, May 20, 1794.

21. R. Jullien to Jullien fils, May 21, 1794.

22. R. Jullien to Jullien fils, June 26, 1792.

23. R. Jullien to Jullien fils, Dec. 24, 1792.

24. R. Jullien to Jullien fils, Nov. 9, 1793.

25. R. Jullien to Jullien fils, July 30, 1794.

26. Palmer, *From Jacobin to Liberal*, 66.

27. R. Jullien to Jullien fils, Aug. 13, 1794.

28. R. Jullien to unknown, Aug. 15, 1794.

29. R. Jullien to unknown, Aug. 16, 1794.

30. R. Jullien to unknown, Aug. 29, 1794.
31. R. Jullien to Tallien, Aug. 18, 1795.
32. Ibid.
33. Ibid.
34. Ibid.
35. R. Jullien to Jullien fils, Mar. 29, 1802.
36. R. Jullien to Jullien fils, Oct. 4, 1802.

CHAPTER 7

1. R. Jullien to Jullien fils, May 7, 1798.
2. For information on Babeuf's beliefs, see Ian H. Birchall, "When the Revolution Had to Stop," in *The French Experience from Republic to Monarchy, 1792–1824: New Dawns in Politics, Knowledge, and Culture,* ed. Máire F. Cross and David Williams (New York: Palgrave, 2000).
3. R. Jullien to Jullien fils, May 7, 1798.
4. Archives nationales, Paris, 39 AP, 1.1.10.
5. Palmer, *From Jacobin to Liberal,* 91.
6. R. Jullien to Jullien fils, Sept. 7, 1800.
7. R. Jullien to Jullien fils, Aug. 19, 1800.
8. R. Jullien to Jullien fils, Nov. 20, 1800.
9. R. Jullien to V. Jullien, Feb. 22, 1801.
10. Ibid.
11. R. Jullien to Jullien fils, Oct. 7, 1801.
12. R. Jullien to Jullien père, July 22, 1801.
13. R. Jullien to Jullien père, Sept. 30, 1801.
14. R. Jullien to Jullien fils, Oct. 7, 1801.
15. R. Jullien to Jullien fils, Feb. 15, 1802.
16. R. Jullien to Jullien fils, Dec. 1, 1800.
17. R. Jullien to Jullien fils, Feb. 22, 1802.
18. R. Jullien to Jullien fils, Jan. 1, 1803.
19. R. Jullien to Jullien fils, Jan. 18, 1803.
20. R. Jullien to Jullien père, Oct. 15, 1801.
21. R. Jullien to V. Jullien, Jan. 9, 1807.
22. R. Jullien to V. Jullien, Nov. 20, 1807.
23. R. Jullien to Jullien fils, July 1, 1803.
24. Jullien père to V. Jullien, Aug. 28, 1803.

25. R. Jullien to Jullien fils, Sept. 5, 1805.

26. R. Jullien to V. Jullien, Apr. 5, 1804.

27. R. Jullien to Jullien père, Sept. 24, 1804.

28. R. Jullien to V. Jullien, July 13, 1803.

29. R. Jullien to V. Jullien, Oct. 10, 1807.

30. R. Jullien to V. Jullien, Feb. 9, 1809.

31. R. Jullien to Jullien fils, Feb. 22, 1802.

32. The records reveal some discrepancies about Stéphanie's birth date. Rosalie's letters about the birth, naming Stéphanie, are dated 1807, and that date corresponds with an event that Rosalie also mentions, the Treaty of Tilsit. But Stéphanie's gravestone places her birth in 1811. A letter that is not dated but that accompanies letters from 1812 from Sophie to Rosalie mentions Stéphanie getting her first tooth. I was unable to locate a birth certificate.

33. For a discussion of medical understandings of sexed bodies, see Thomas Laqueur, *Making Sex: Body and Gender from the Greeks to Freud* (Cambridge, MA: Harvard University Press, 1990).

34. R. Jullien to S. Jullien, Feb. 25, 1802.

35. R. Jullien to Jullien fils, Feb. 22, 1802.

36. R. Jullien to S. Jullien, Feb. 25, 1802.

37. R. Jullien to Jullien fils, Dec. 8, 1802.

38. R. Jullien to Jullien fils, Apr. 12, 1802.

39. R. Jullien to Jullien fils, Feb. 15, 1803.

40. R. Jullien to Jullien fils, Jan. 18, 1805.

41. R. Jullien to Jullien fils, Feb. 22, 1802. Robert Nye suggests that after the Revolution, men were reminded of "the fragile nature of their authority," and one result of this was that "sexual potency had become a crucial concept for thinking about power." Nye, *Masculinity and Male Codes of Honor*, 49.

42. R. Jullien to V. Jullien, July 28, 1805. For a description of early modern labor and delivery practices, see Gelbart, *The King's Midwife*.

43. R. Jullien to V. Jullien, June 1, 1807.

44. R. Jullien to S. Jullien, Oct. 22, 1808.

45. R. Jullien to Jullien fils, June 8, 1804.

46. R. Jullien to S. Jullien, June 13, 1804.

47. Jullien père to Jullien fils, June 22, 1804.

48. R. Jullien to Jullien fils, June 22, 1804

49. R. Jullien to Jullien fils, June 25, 1804.

50. R. Jullien to Jullien fils, Apr. 24, 1802.

51. Ibid.

52. Ibid.

53. R. Jullien to Jullien fils, Sept. 17, 1802.

54. R. Jullien to Jullien fils, Apr. 24, 1802.

55. R. Jullien to V. Jullien, Nov. 4, 1807.

56. Yves-Marie Bercé, *Le chaudron et la lancette: Croyances populaires et méde-cine préventive, 1798–1830* (Paris: Presses de la Renaissance, 1984), 80.

57. Ibid., 108.

58. R. Jullien to Jullien fils, Sept. 27, 1802.

59. R. Jullien to Jullien fils, July 30, 1802.

60. R. Jullien to Jullien fils, Aug. 7, 1802.

61. R. Jullien to Jullien fils, Aug. 2, 1802.

62. R. Jullien to Jullien fils, May 31, 1803.

63. David M. Vess, *Medical Revolution in France, 1789–1796* (Gainesville: University Presses of Florida, 1975).

64. Bercé, *Le chaudron et la lancette*.

65. Jullien père to Nugues père, 1780, private collection.

66. R. Jullien to C. Nugues, 1783, private collection.

67. Christine Adams also notes a "constant admonition to 'watch your purse'" in the Lamothe family letters from the mid-eighteenth century. Adams, *Taste for Comfort*, 20.

68. R. Jullien to Jullien fils, Sept. 21, 1803.

69. R. Jullien to Jullien fils, Jan. 5, 1808.

70. R. Jullien to Jullien fils, Mar. 16, 1804.

71. Again, the Julliens share this quality with the Lamothe family. Adams writes: "In this, the Lamothes imitated other professional and bourgeois families in France, and manifested once again their fundamentally conservative nature. The eighteenth-century Frenchman or -woman was most likely to invest in proprietary wealth, that is, land, *rentes*, and offices. These types of investments provided relatively low returns, but were low risk and very stable." Adams, *Taste for Comfort*, 67–68.

72. R. Jullien to Jullien fils, Mar. 16, 1804.

73. R. Jullien to V. Jullien, Apr. 5, 1804.

74. R. Jullien to Jullien fils, Sept. 7, 1800.

75. R. Jullien to Jullien fils, Sept. 21, 1803.

76. R. Jullien to Jullien fils, May 21, 1803.

77. R. Jullien to Jullien fils, Oct. 21, 1802.

78. R. Jullien to V. Jullien, July 17, 1805.

79. Garrioch, *Formation of the Parisian Bourgeoisie*, 281.

80. David Garrioch argues that the Revolution firmly concluded a process that had begun earlier in the eighteenth century, in which old hierarchies—family lineages, authority from religious affiliations, and guilds—were broken down to permit the ascendance of the bourgeoisie into politically powerful positions. Garrioch and Robert Nye suggest that the Revolution created the bourgeoisie when, in Nye's words, "the values central to bourgeois social reproduction were enshrined in the nation's laws and embedded in its institutions." Ibid., 143–44, 174; Nye, *Masculinity and Male Codes of Honor*, 47.

81. R. Jullien to Jullien fils, May 5, 1803.

82. R. Jullien to Jullien fils, Sept. 28, 1802.

83. R. Jullien to Jullien fils, Sept. 21, 1803.

84. Like the Julliens, the Lamothe family "placed strong emphasis on personal values, including family ties, religious devotion, self-restraint, and domestic comfort, and highly valued their stable and family-centered existence." They also included in their correspondence the "constant admonition to 'watch your purse'" and endorsed "efforts to maintain a moderate lifestyle." Adams, *Taste for Comfort*, 19–20, 31.

85. R. Jullien to V. Jullien, July 18, 1801.

86. R. Jullien to Jullien fils, Sept. 7, 1800.

87. R. Jullien to Jullien fils, Aug. 28, 1805.

88. R. Jullien to S. Jullien, June 13, 1804; R. Jullien to V. Jullien, May 14, 1804.

89. R. Jullien to Jullien fils, Aug. 24, 1808.

90. R. Jullien to Jullien fils, Sept. 11, 1809.

CONCLUSION

1. Heuer, *The Family and the Nation*, 131.

2. Hufton, *Women and the Limits of Citizenship*; Proctor, *Women, Equality, and the French Revolution*.

3. Denise Davidson, *France after Revolution: Urban Life, Gender, and the New Social Order* (Cambridge, MA: Harvard University Press, 2007).

4. Joan Wallach Scott, "French Feminists and the Rights of 'Man': Olympe de Gouges's Declarations," *History Workshop* 28 (Fall 1989): 5.

5. Marisa Linton notes that this ambiguity is typical of the period because of competing notions of women's virtue in Christian, humanist, and Enlightenment discourse. Linton, "Virtue Rewarded?"

6. Bonnie Smith argues that by the mid-nineteenth century, men and women would inhabit a "world apart" from each other. Smith, *Ladies of the Leisure Class.*

7. R. Jullien to Jullien fils, Aug. 4, 1802.

8. R. Jullien to Jullien fils, Feb. 15, 1802.

9. R. Jullien to Jullien fils, Sept. 19, 1803.

10. R. Jullien to Jullien fils, Oct. 26, 1802.

11. R. Jullien to Jullien fils, June 11, 1803.

12. In other places, women stood for the demise of republicanism; in Rosalie's writing they were the vaults of republican virtue. Olwen Hufton argues that "the most persistent ghost of the French Revolution was…hysterical, perverse, irrational, unreliable Eve," who "kept [man] from earthly paradise" in the Republic. Hufton, *Women and the Limits of Citizenship*, 154. The ghost of a revolutionary woman in Rosalie's prose is patient and obscured and more prepared for a successful revolution than her male counterparts.

13. R. Jullien to Jullien fils, May 29, 1794.

14. R. Jullien to Jullien fils, Oct. 1, 1802.

15. May, *Madame Roland and the Age of Revolution*; Reynolds, *Marriage and Revolution.*

16. Cole, *Between the Queen and the Cabby.*

17. Elizabeth C. Goldsmith, ed., *Writing the Female Voice: Essays on Epistolary Literature* (Boston: Northeastern University Press, 1989).

18. But it could be. See Caroline Bland and Máire Cross, eds., *Gender and Politics in the Age of Letter-Writing, 1750–2000* (Burlington, VT: Ashgate, 2004).

19. Carla Hesse, *The Other Enlightenment: How French Women Became Modern* (Princeton, NJ: Princeton University Press, 2001), xii.

20. In this argument, I support Dena Goodman's thesis: "[T]here is more to modernity than the public and the political. Privateness, too, was novel in the eighteenth century; intimacy, we are told, was 'invented' then.… The very possibility of coming together with others to form a public was

predicated on this prior sense of oneself as a private person, achieved through cultural practices such as letter writing that developed interiority and reflection." Goodman, *Becoming a Woman*, 4.

21. Jullien fils to Simon Lockroy, Feb. 14, 1837.
22. Jullien fils to Stéphanie Lockroy, Aug. 1, 1840.
23. R. Jullien to Jullien père, Aug. 28, 1801.
24. R. Jullien to Jullien fils, June 1, 1792.
25. R. Jullien to Jullien fils, Jan. 1, 1803.
26. R. Jullien to Jullien fils, Feb. 20, 1804.

Bibliography

Adams, Christine. *A Taste for Comfort and Status: A Bourgeois Family in Eighteenth-Century France*. University Park: Pennsylvania State University Press, 2000.

Altman, Janet Gurkin. *Epistolarity: Approaches to a Form*. Columbus: Ohio State University Press, 1982.

———. "The Letter Book as a Literary Institution 1539–1789: Toward a Cultural History of Published Correspondences in France." *Yale French Studies* 71 (special issue 1986): 17–62.

Baker, Keith Michael. *Inventing the French Revolution: Essays on French Political Culture in the Eighteenth Century*. Cambridge: Cambridge University Press, 1990.

———. "A Script for a French Revolution: The Political Consciousness of the Abbé Mably." *Eighteenth-Century Studies* 14, no. 3 (Spring 1981): 235–63.

Beckstrand, Lisa. *Deviant Women of the French Revolution and the Rise of Feminism*. Madison, NJ: Fairleigh Dickinson University Press, 2009.

Beizer, Janet. *Thinking through the Mothers: Reimagining Women's Biographies*. Ithaca, NY: Cornell University Press, 2009.

Bell, David. *The Cult of the Nation in France: Inventing Nationalism, 1680–1800*. Cambridge, MA: Harvard University Press, 2001.

Bercé, Yves-Marie. *Le chaudron et la lancette: Croyances populaires et médecine préventive, 1798–1830*. Paris: Presses de la Renaissance, 1984.

Birchall, Ian H. "When the Revolution Had to Stop." In *The French Experience from Republic to Monarchy, 1792–1824: New Dawns in Politics, Knowledge, and Culture*, edited by Máire F. Cross and David Williams. New York: Palgrave, 2000.

Bland, Caroline, and Máire Cross, eds. *Gender and Politics in the Age of Letter-Writing, 1750–2000.* Burlington, VT: Ashgate, 2004.

Bossis, Mireille. "Methodological Journeys through Correspondences." *Yale French Studies* 71 (special issue 1986): 643–75.

Brunel, Georges. *La poste à Paris depuis sa creation jusqu'à mos jours, etude historique et anecdotique.* Amiens: Yvert & Teller, 1920.

Censer, Jack. *Prelude to Power: The Parisian Radical Press, 1789–1791.* Baltimore, MD: Johns Hopkins University Press, 1976.

Chartier, Roger. *The Cultural Origins of the French Revolution.* Translated by Lydia G. Cochrane. Durham, NC: Duke University Press, 1991.

Choudhury, Mita. *Convents and Nuns in Eighteenth-Century French Politics and Culture.* Ithaca, NY: Cornell University Press, 2004.

Cole, John R. *Between the Queen and the Cabby: Olympe de Gouges's "Rights of Woman."* New York: McGill-Queen's University Press, 2011.

Culoma, Michael. *La religion civile de Rousseau à Robespierre.* Paris: L'Harmattan, 2010.

Darnton, Robert. *The Great Cat Massacre and Other Episodes in French Cultural History.* New York: Vintage Books, 1984.

———. "The High Enlightenment and the Low Life of Literature." *Past and Present* 51 (1971): 81–115.

———. "In Search of the Enlightenment: Recent Attempts to Create a Social History of Ideas." *Journal of Modern History* 43, no. 1 (1971): 113–32.

Darrow, Margaret. "French Noblewomen and the New Domesticity, 1750–1850." *Feminist Studies* 5, no. 1 (Spring 1979): 41–65.

———. "Popular Concepts of Marital Choice in Eighteenth-Century France." *Journal of Social History* 19, no. 2 (Winter 1985): 261–72.

———. *Revolution in the House: Family, Class, and Inheritance in Southern France, 1775–1825.* Princeton, NJ: Princeton University Press, 1989.

Davidson, Denise. *France after Revolution: Urban Life, Gender, and the New Social Order.* Cambridge, MA: Harvard University Press, 2007.

Debauve, Jean-Louis. "A propos de Marc-Antoine Jullien et de la Société polymathique [du Morbihan]." *Bulletin de la Société Polymathique Morbihan,* P.-V. 108 (1981): 43–45.

Desan, Suzanne. "Constitutional Amazons." In *Re-creating Authority in Revolutionary France,* edited by Bryant T. Ragan, Jr., and Elizabeth A. Williams. New Brunswick, NJ: Rutgers University Press, 1992.

———. *The Family on Trial in Revolutionary France.* Berkeley: University of California Press, 2004.

Diaz, Brigitte. *L'épistolaire ou la pensée nomade: Formes et functions de la correspondance dans quelques parcours d'écrivains au XIXe siècle.* Paris: Presses Universitaires de France, 2002.

Diaz, Brigitte, and Jürgen Siess, eds. *L'épistolaire au féminin: Correspondances de femmes (XVIIe–XXe siècle).* Caen: Presses Universitaires de Caen, 2006.

Diderot, Denis, and Claude Yvon. "Friendship." In *The Encyclopedia of Diderot & d'Alembert Collaborative Translation Project,* translated by Jeffrey Merrick. Ann Arbor: MPublishing, University of Michigan Library, 2003, http://hdl.handle.net/2027/spo.did2222.0000.182 (accessed May 1, 2012). Originally published as "Amitié." In *Encyclopédie ou dictionnaire raisonné des sciences, des arts et des métiers,* 1:361–62 (Paris, 1751).

Earle, Rebecca, ed. *Epistolary Selves: Letters and Letter-Writers, 1600–1945.* Burlington, VT: Ashgate, 1999.

Fairchilds, Cissie. *Domestic Enemies: Servants and Their Masters in Old Regime France.* Baltimore: Johns Hopkins University Press, 1984.

Farrell, Michèle Longino. *Performing Motherhood: The Sévigné Correspondence.* Hanover, NH: University Press of New England, 1991.

Flandrin, Jean-Louis. *Families in Former Times: Kinship, Household and Sexuality.* Translated by Richard Southern. New York: Cambridge University Press, 1979.

Furet, François. *Interpreting the French Revolution.* Translated by Elborg Forster. Paris: Editions de la Maison des Sciences de l'Homme, 1988.

Garrioch, David. "The Everyday Lives of Parisian Women and the October Days of 1789." *Social History* 24, no. 3 (October 1999): 231–49.

———. *The Formation of the Parisian Bourgeoisie, 1690–1830.* Cambridge, MA: Harvard University Press, 1996.

———. *The Making of Revolutionary Paris.* Berkeley: University of California Press, 2002.

Gascar, Pierre. *L'ombre de Robespierre.* Paris: Gallimard, 1979.

Gay, Peter. *The Enlightenment: An Interpretation.* New York: Knopf, 1966.

Gelbart, Nina Rattner. *Feminism and Opposition Journalism in Old Regime France: Le Journal des Dames.* Berkeley: University of California Press, 1986.

———. *The King's Midwife: A History and Mystery of Madame du Coudray.* Berkeley: University of California Press, 1998.

Gelfand, Elissa D. *Imagination in Confinement: Women's Writings from French Prisons.* Ithaca, NY: Cornell University Press, 1983.

Giraud, Jean. "Marc-Antoine Jullien de Paris." *Paedagogica Historica* 15, no. 2 (1975): 379–405.

Godineau, Dominique. *The Women of Paris and Their French Revolution.* Translated by Katherine Streip. Berkeley: University of California Press, 1988.

Goetz, Helmut. *Marc-Antoine Jullien de Paris (1775–1848): L'évolution spirituelle d'un révolutionnaire.* Paris: Institut pédagogique national, 1962.

Goldsmith, Elizabeth C., ed. *Writing the Female Voice: Essays on Epistolary Literature.* Boston: Northeastern University Press, 1989.

Goldstein, Jan. *The Post-revolutionary Self: Politics and Psyche in France, 1750–1850.* Cambridge, MA: Harvard University Press, 2005.

Goodman, Dena. *Becoming a Woman in the Age of Letters.* Ithaca, NY: Cornell University Press, 2009.

———. "Letter Writing and the Emergence of Gendered Subjectivity in Eighteenth-Century France." *Journal of Women's History* 17, no. 2 (2005): 9–37.

———. "L'Ortografe des Dames: Gender and Language in the Old Regime." *French Historical Studies* 25, no. 2 (2002): 191–223.

———. *The Republic of Letters: A Cultural History of the French Enlightenment.* Ithaca, NY: Cornell University Press, 1994.

Gordon, Felicia. "The Gendered Citizen: Marie Madeleine Jodin (1741–90)." In *The French Experience from Republic to Monarchy, 1792–1824: New Dawns in Politics, Knowledge, and Culture,* edited by Máire F. Cross and David Williams. New York: Palgrave, 2000.

Grassi, Marie-Claire. *L'art de la lettre au temps de "La nouvelle Héloïse" et du romantisme.* Geneva: Slatkine, 1994.

———. "Friends and Lovers (or the Codification of Intimacy)." *Yale French Studies* 71 (special issue 1986): 77–92.

Gross, Jean-Pierre. *Fair Shares for All: Jacobin Egalitarianism in Practice.* New York: Cambridge University Press, 1997.

Gutwirth, Madelyn. *The Twilight of the Goddesses: Women and Representation in the French Revolutionary Era.* New Brunswick, NJ: Rutgers University Press, 1992.

Hampson, Norman. "Mably and the Montagnards." *French History* 16, no. 4 (2002): 402–15.

Hanson, Paul. *The Jacobin Republic under Fire: The Federalist Revolt in the French Revolution.* University Park: Pennsylvania State University Press, 2003.

Haydon, Colin, and William Doyle, eds. *Robespierre.* Cambridge: Cambridge University Press, 1999.

Hesse, Carla. *The Other Enlightenment: How French Women Became Modern.* Princeton, NJ: Princeton University Press, 2001.

Heuer, Jennifer. *The Family and the Nation: Gender and Citizenship in Revolutionary France, 1789–1830.* Ithaca, NY: Cornell University Press, 2005.

Hirschmann, Nancy. *The Subject of Liberty: Toward a Feminist Theory of Freedom.* Princeton, NJ: Princeton University Press, 2003.

Holowach, Lindsay. "L'éveil d'une conscience féminine au cours de la Revolution française: Rosalie Jullien (1785–1792)." In *Colloque Archive epistolaire et Histoire,* edited by Mireille Bossis and Lucia Bergamasco. Paris: Connaissances et Savoirs, 2007.

Hufton, Olwen. *The Prospect before Her: A History of Women in Western Europe, 1500–1800.* New York: Vintage Books, 1998.

———. "Voilà la Citoyenne." *History Today* 39, no. 5 (May 1989): 26–32.

———. *Women and the Limits of Citizenship in the French Revolution.* Toronto: University of Toronto Press, 1992.

Hunt, Lynn. *The Family Romance of the French Revolution.* Berkeley: University of California Press, 1992.

———. "Hercules and the Radical Image in the French Revolution." *Representations 2* (Spring 1983): 95–117.

Jacob, Margaret. *Living the Enlightenment: Freemasonry and Politics in Eighteenth-Century Europe.* New York: Oxford University Press, 1991.

Jordan, David. *The King's Trial: The French Revolution vs. Louis XVI.* Berkeley: University of California Press, 1979.

Jullien, Rosalie. *Journal d'une bourgeoise pendant la Révolution française.* Edited by Edouard Lockroy. Paris: C. Lévy, 1881.

Kermina, Françoise. *Madame Tallien.* Paris: Perrin, 2006.

Krakovitch, Odile. "Un cas de censure familiale: La correspondance revue et corrigée de Rosalie Jullien (1789–1793) [par Edouard Lockroy, son arrière-petit-fils]." *Histoire et Archive* 9 (2001): 81–123.

Landes, Joan. *Women and the Public Sphere in the Age of the French Revolution.* Ithaca, NY: Cornell University Press, 1988.

Lange, Lynda. "Rousseau and Modern Feminism." In *Feminist Interpretations of Jean-Jacques Rousseau,* edited by Lynda Lange. University Park: Pennsylvania State University Press, 2002.

Laqueur, Thomas. *Making Sex: Body and Gender from the Greeks to Freud.* Cambridge, MA: Harvard University Press, 1990.

Lefebvre, Georges. *The Coming of the French Revolution.* Translated by R. R. Palmer. Princeton, NJ: Princeton University Press, 1975.

Lejeune, Philippe. "Marc-Antoine Jullien: Contrôleur de temps." *Lalies* 28 (2008): 205–20.

Lepore, Jill. "Historians Who Love Too Much: Reflections on Microhistory and Biography." *Journal of American History* 88 (2001): 129–44.

Levi, Giovanni. "Les usages de la biographie." *Annales: Economies, Sociétés, Civilisations* 6 (November/December 1989): 1325–36.

Levy, Darlene Gay. "Women's Revolutionary Citizenship in Action, 1791: Setting the Boundaries." In *The French Revolution and the Meaning of Citizenship,* edited by Renée Waldinger, Philip Dawson, and Isser Woloch. Westport, CT: Greenwood Press, 1993.

Linton, Marisa. "Fatal Friendships: The Politics of Jacobin Friendship." *French Historical Studies* 31, no. 1 (Winter 2008): 51–76.

———. *The Politics of Virtue in Enlightenment France.* New York: Palgrave, 2001.

———. "Virtue Rewarded? Women and the Politics of Virtue in 18th-Century France. Part I." *History of European Ideas* 26, no. 1 (2000): 35–49.

Margadant, Jo Burr, ed. *The New Biography: Performing Femininity in Nineteenth-Century France.* Berkeley: University of California Press, 2000.

Markoff, John. "Images of the King at the Beginning of the Revolution." In *Revolutionary Demands: A Content Analysis of the Cahiers de Doléances of 1789,* edited by Gilbert Shapiro and John Markoff. Stanford, CA: Stanford University Press, 1997.

Martin, Jean-Clément. *Contre-révolution, révolution et nation en France: 1789–1799.* Paris: Editions du Seuil, 1998.

———. *La révolte brisée: Femmes dans la Révolution française et l'Empire.* Paris: Armand Colin, 2008.

May, Gita. *Madame Roland and the Age of Revolution.* New York: Columbia University Press, 1970.

Mayer, Arno. *The Furies: Violence and Terror in the French and Russian Revolutions*. Princeton, NJ: Princeton University Press, 2000.

Maza, Sarah. *The Myth of the French Bourgeoisie: An Essay on the Social Imaginary, 1750–1850*. Cambridge, MA: Harvard University Press, 2003.

———. *Private Lives and Public Affairs: The Causes Célèbres of Prerevolutionary France*. Berkeley: University of California Press, 1993.

McAlpin, Mary. *Gender, Authenticity, and the Missive Letter in Eighteenth-Century France: Marie-Anne de La Tour, Rousseau's Real-Life Julie*. Lewisburg, PA: Bucknell University Press, 2006.

Montesquieu, Charles de Secondat, baron de. *The Persian Letters*. Translated by Margaret Mauldon. New York: Oxford University Press, 2008.

Moote, Lloyd. "New Bottles and New Wine: The Current State of Early Modernist Biographical Writing." *French Historical Studies* 19, no. 4 (Autumn 1996): 911–26.

Mornet, Daniel. *Les origines intellectuelles de la Révolution française*. Paris: A. Colin, 1954.

Nye, Robert A. *Masculinity and Male Codes of Honor in Modern France*. New York: Oxford University Press, 1993.

O'Day, Rosemary. *The Family and Family Relationships, 1500–1900: England, France, and the United States of America*. New York: St. Martin's Press, 1994.

Outram, Dorinda. *The Body and the French Revolution: Sex, Class and Political Culture*. New Haven, CT: Yale University Press, 1989.

Ozouf, Mona. *Festivals and the French Revolution*. Translated by Alan Sheridan. Cambridge, MA: Harvard University Press, 1988.

Palmer, Robert R. *From Jacobin to Liberal: Marc-Antoine Jullien, 1775–1848*. Princeton, NJ: Princeton University Press, 1993.

———. *Twelve Who Ruled: The Year of Terror in the French Revolution*. Princeton, NJ: Princeton University Press, 1941.

Parker, Lindsay A. H. "Family and Feminism in the French Revolution: The Case of Rosalie Ducrollay Jullien." *Journal of Women's History* 24, no. 3 (Fall 2012): 39–61.

———. "Veiled Emotions: Rosalie Jullien and the Politics of Feeling in the French Revolution." *Journal of Historical Biography*, forthcoming.

Pateman, Carole. *The Sexual Contract*. Cambridge: Polity Press, 1988.

Pierre, Roger, et al. *240.000 Drômois: La fin de l'ancien régime les débuts de la Révolution*. Valence: Notre Temps, 1989.

Popkin, Jeremy. *Revolutionary News: The Press in France, 1789–1799*. Durham, NC: Duke University Press, 1990.

Poster, Carol, and Linda C. Mitchell, eds. *Letter-Writing Manuals and Instruction from Antiquity to the Present: Historical and Bibliographic Studies*. Columbia: University of South Carolina Press, 2007.

Proctor, Candice. *Women, Equality, and the French Revolution*. New York: Greenwood Press, 1990.

Reddy, William M. *The Navigation of Feeling: A Framework for the History of Emotions*. Cambridge: Cambridge University Press, 2001.

Reynolds, Siân. *Marriage and Revolution: Monsieur and Madame Roland*. Oxford: Oxford University Press, 2012.

Robiquet, Jean. *Daily Life in the French Revolution*. Translated by James Kirkup. New York: Macmillan, 1965.

Rousseau, Jean-Jacques. *Emile*. Translated by Barbara Foxley. http://www.gutenberg.org/ebooks/5427.

Rudé, George. *The Crowd in the French Revolution*. Oxford: Clarendon Press, 1959.

Schiebinger, Londa. "Why Mammals Are Called Mammals: Gender Politics in Eighteenth-Century Natural History." *American Historical Review* 98, no. 2 (April 1993): 382–411.

Scott, Joan Wallach. "French Feminists and the Rights of 'Man': Olympe de Gouges's Declarations." *History Workshop* 28 (Fall 1989): 1–21.

———. *Only Paradoxes to Offer: French Feminists and the Rights of Man*. Cambridge, MA: Harvard University Press, 1996.

Scott, Joan Wallach, and Debra Keates, eds. *Going Public: Feminism and the Shifting Boundaries of the Private Sphere*. Urbana: University of Illinois Press, 2004.

Servan, Joseph Michel Antoine. *Reflexions sur les Confessions de J. J. Rousseau*. Paris: [H.-E. Vincent], 1783.

Shorter, Edward. "Illegitimacy, Sexual Revolution, and Social Change in Modern Europe." *Journal of Interdisciplinary History* 2, no. 2 (1971): 237–72.

Shovlin, John. *The Political Economy of Virtue: Luxury, Patriotism, and the Origins of the French Revolution*. Ithaca, NY: Cornell University Press, 2006.

Smith, Bonnie G. *Ladies of the Leisure Class: The Bourgeoises of Northern France in the Nineteenth Century*. Princeton, NJ: Princeton University Press, 1981.

Soboul, Albert. *The Parisian Sans-Culottes and the French Revolution 1793–4.* Translated by Gwynne Lewis. Oxford: Clarendon Press, 1964.

Sussman, George D. *Selling Mothers' Milk: The Wet-Nursing Business in France, 1715–1914.* Urbana: University of Illinois Press, 1982.

Tackett, Timothy. *Becoming a Revolutionary: The Deputies of the French National Assembly and the Emergence of a Revolutionary Culture (1789–1790).* Princeton, NJ: Princeton University Press, 1996.

———. "Conspiracy Obsession in a Time of Revolution: French Elites and the Origins of the Terror, 1789–1792." *American Historical Review* 105, no. 3 (June 2000): 691–713.

———. "Paths to Revolution: The Old Regime Correspondence of Five Future Revolutionaries." *French Historical Studies* 32, no. 4 (Fall 2009): 531–54.

———. *Priest and Parish in Eighteenth-Century France.* Princeton, NJ: Princeton University Press, 1977.

———. "The West in France in 1789: The Religious Factor in the Origins of the Counterrevolution." *Journal of Modern History* 54, no. 5 (December 1992): 715–45.

———. *When the King Took Flight.* Cambridge, MA: Harvard University Press, 2003.

Tilly, Louise A., and Joan W. Scott. *Women, Work, and Family.* New York: Holt, Rinehart and Winston, 1978.

Vargas, Pierre. "L'éducation du 'petit Jullien' agent du Comité de Salut public." In *L'enfant, la famille et la Révolution française*, edited by Marie-Françoise Lévy. Paris: Olivier Orban, 1990.

———. "L'héritage de Marc-Antoine Jullien, de Paris à Moscou." *Annales historiques de la Révolution française* 301 (1995): 409–31.

Verjus, Anne. *Le bon mari: Une histoire politique des hommes et des femmes à l'époque révolutionaire.* Paris: Fayard, 2010.

Verjus, Anne, and Denise Davidson. *Le Roman conjugal: Chroniques de la vie familiale à l'époque de la Révolution et de l'Empire.* Seyssel: Champ Vallon, 2011.

Vess, David M. *Medical Revolution in France, 1789–1796.* Gainesville: University Presses of Florida, 1975.

Weiss, Penny, and Anne Harper. "Rousseau's Political Defense of the Sex-Roled Family." In *Feminist Interpretations of Jean-Jacques Rousseau*, edited by Lynda Lange. University Park: Pennsylvania State University Press, 2002.

Index

Nantes, the *noyades* at, 96–97
Naples, 121, 143
Napoleonic Code, 4, 5, 141
National Convention, and Marc-
    Antoine, 83–84
National Guard, 52
Nioche, Pierre-Claude, 122
Nugues
    family, 20, 21, 22, 23, 44, 45, 130–32
    Saint-Cyr, 22–23, 57–58, 69, 95–96, 97
nuns, 59
nursing
    maternal, 127, 129–30
    and Rousseau, 34, 37–40, 130
    See also wet nurse

Oath, Tennis Court, 49, 70
October Days, 50, 54–55
opium, 124, 125

parenting, 105–7
    See also Rousseau, on parenting
passive citizens, 4, 88, 142
Père Lachaise, 1, 147, 148
Pétion, Jérôme, 62, 63, 69, 72, 115
Phedre, 24
Phlipon, Manon, 41
    See also Roland, Madame
Pontoise, 2, 11, 64, 73
post, 67
pregnancy, 16, 23, 126–28
priests. *See* clergy
Prieur of the Marne, 97
Prussia, war with, 90

Quakers, 85

Racine, 28, 32
Republican Mother, 4, 37–38, 40, 117, 145
rheumatism, 124
Richardson, Samuel, 41–43
Robespierre, Maximilen, 3, 62, 63, 91, 93,
    94, 97, 98, 116

Roland, Madame, 5, 28, 111, 144
    See also Phlipon, Manon
Rome, ancient, allusions to, 42, 65, 73,
    74, 92, 93
Romme, Gilbert, 105
Rousseau, Jean-Jacques
    and Marc-Antoine, 2, 31–34, 63
    on parenting, 24–27, 29, 34, 37
    and Rosalie, 37, 41, 116
    on the social contract, 33, 93, 112
    on women, 103, 147
    See also marriage, companionate; nurs-
        ing, and Rousseau

Saint-André, Jean Bòn, 97
Saint Bartholomew's Day Massacre, 70
Saint-Germain, 20, 53, 75
sansculottes, 54, 70, 79, 105
sciatica, 125
September Massacres, 80–82
Servan, Joseph, 31–32, 45, 89
servants, domestic, 19, 133
Sieyès, abbé, 51
silk worms, 19, 47
smallpox, 16, 23
    See also vaccine
Society of Republican Revolutionary
    Women. *See* women, political clubs
St. Just, 97
St. Malo, 105, 107
Stanhope, Lord, 35, 69, 85

Tallien, Jean-Lambert, 96, 115, 117, 118
Tallien, Thérésa, 118–19
Tarbes, 89, 91
the Terror, ideology of, 98, 100, 101, 110
Tiberge, Mademoiselle, 16, 18, 20, 22, 25,
    42, 63

United States, 32

vaccine, smallpox, 131–33
Vendée, 60, 90, 103

Printed in the USA/Agawam, MA
June 13, 2014

591047.058